'I Thirst'

'I Thirst'

The Cross — The Great Triumph of Love

Stephen Cottrell

Foreword by the Archbishop of Canterbury

ZONDERVAN™

GRAND RAPIDS, MICHIGAN 49530 USA

Library of Congress Cataloging-in-Publication Data

Cottrell, Stephen.
   I thirst : the cross—the great triumph of love / Stephen Cottrell
      p. cm.
   Includes bibliographical references.
   ISBN 0-310-25069-2
   1. Jesus Christ—Crucifixion.   I. Title.
BT453.C65 2003
232.96'35—dc21   2003014015
                                                         CIP

Interior design by Beth Shagene

Printed and bound in the United Kingdom

---

03 04 05 06 07 08 09 /❖ CLY/ 10 9 8 7 6 5 4 3 2 1

For Rebecca

Contents

After this, when Jesus knew that all was now finished, he said (in order to fulfil the scripture), 'I am thirsty.' A jar full of sour wine was standing there. So they put a sponge full of the wine on a branch of hyssop and held it to his mouth. When Jesus had received the wine, he said, 'It is finished.' Then he bowed his head and gave up his spirit.

JOHN 19:28–30

Foreword by the Archbishop of Canterbury

On the wall at the end of the dining room at a well-known convent in Oxford is a simple crucifix, with underneath it the single Latin word, *Sitio*, 'I thirst'. It reminds the sisters each time they gather that Christ looks to us to respond to his thirst for our life and healing, our prayer and love. In this book, Stephen Cottrell explores that divine thirst – the love so insistent that it can only appear as the deepest vulnerability. You can read this, in fact, as an introduction to almost every aspect of Christian belief overall, since there is very little here that does not cast fresh light on the whole pattern of doctrine.

But as well as being so far-reaching, it is also a movingly personal book, and a practical one. It shows something of the cost of conversion – the difference made by Jesus to us in our thinking and acting. So, as he says, it is an introduction to the main practices of Christian discipline, fasting and prayer and Bible reading, in such a way that they appear new, exciting and challenging. Stephen is clear that our Christian faith has to be lived in the small particulars, and some of the best pages here are those which describe what conversion might look like in practice. How much water do we use boiling kettles and flushing loos each day, in a world where water is becoming desperately scarce? How much attention do we give to the small task of making someone else's bed? This is where conversion begins to mean something.

Stephen writes out of the experience of some years as an animator of mission around the country; indeed, few have quite his range of awareness of the varieties of 'ordinary' church life. We are very lucky to have from him so readable, so compelling and so helpful a book, the fruit of much deeply meditated sharing of the good news with people of all sorts. Reading it is a real rediscovery of the fresh waters of faith.

† Rowan Cantuar

Archbishop of Canterbury

Introduction

For five years in the late 1980s and early 1990s I had the great privilege of serving as parish priest of St Wilfrid's, Chichester. While I was there we acquired a new cross for the church. Well, not really a new one: a friend of mine, Fr Martin Warner, knew of a religious community that was moving premises and no longer had use for a crucifix, which could be ours for a small sum. It was no great work of art, but we felt its simple depiction of Jesus would add something to our church building. Of course, not all Christians are comfortable with the imagery of a crucifix, and prefer a plain empty cross. But a crucifix does help us conceptualize the story of Christ's passion.

The crucifix duly arrived and we hung it in the church on the east wall behind the altar. Then when Martin and I stood looking at it he said to me that whenever he looked at a crucifix, or a painting of the crucifixion, he always wondered which words of Jesus spoken from the cross the artist had in mind. We looked in silence at the sad, tortured figure strung up on the cold, hard wood of the cross, eyes gazing upwards, mouth half open. 'I thirst,' it seemed to be saying. This cross was about the suffering and longing of Jesus, his agony and his love.

And that, I suppose, was when this book began. The following Good Friday I preached on the text from John's

Gospel where the dying Christ cries out, 'I am thirsty,' and told the story of how Martin and I had stood in the church on the day the cross was put up and discussed what it was saying to us. And often, when praying in the church, or bowing before the altar as the Eucharist began, I would think of those words of Christ. They are such sorrowful words, so simple and yet so very human: Christ, the thirsty one, one who shares deeply in the mess and muddle of human living. They are words of desire: not just the physical longing for a drink, but a whole panoply of longing.

Several years later the sermon became a series of short talks to meditate upon the different ways we understand the meaning of the cross. And now it is a book, offered to help us penetrate the deep mystery of a God who goes on loving, no matter how exorbitant the cost, no matter the obstacles put in the way.

The book has six chapters, one for each week of Lent. Each looks at the words 'I thirst' in a different way. In particular, the book follows the passion story in John's Gospel – in fact, the whole book is deeply rooted in the Fourth Gospel, finding there an understanding of the cross as a revelation of God's glory, the great triumph of love.

Each chapter also includes a section on the implications for our lives of viewing the cross in this way, as well as suggestions for group discussion and for prayer.

It is also a book for Lent. This is an important, but often neglected, season in the church year. Lent is supposed to be a time when we review our spiritual life, think again about what it means to be a follower of Christ, reset the compass of our discipleship, and prepare ourselves to celebrate the Easter festival. But often we just give up biscuits.

The order for the beginning of Lent, set to be used by churches on Ash Wednesday, has these words right at the beginning of the service:

> Brothers and sisters in Christ: since early days Christians have observed with great devotion the time of our Lord's passion and resurrection. It became the custom of the church to prepare for this by a season of penitence and fasting.
>
> At first this season of Lent was observed by those who were preparing for Baptism at Easter and by those who were to be restored to the church's fellowship from which they had been separated through sin. In course of time the church came to recognize that, by a careful keeping of these days, all Christians might take to heart the call to repentance and the assurance of forgiveness proclaimed in the gospel, and so grow in faith and in devotion to our Lord.
>
> I invite you, therefore, in the name of the church, to the observance of a holy Lent, by self-examination and repentance; by prayer, fasting, and self-denial; and by reading and meditating on God's holy word.[1]

I add almsgiving to the list above.

One aim of this book is to help us rediscover these traditional Lenten disciplines, to prepare us properly for Holy Week and Easter so that we might grow in 'faith and devotion to our Lord'.

Throughout this book we will explore what the death of Jesus means, and how it relates to our lives today. Week by week, chapter by chapter, we will uncover the layers of meaning in his simple cry of longing 'I thirst.' I pray that, as you read this, you will experience, as if for the first time, the scale and wonder of God's love; and come, at the end of Lent, to the great festival of Easter knowing afresh what it means for God to love you and what it means to serve him in the world.

> The cross is the surest, truest and deepest window on the very heart and character of the living and loving God; the more we learn about the cross, in all its historical and theological dimensions, the more we discover about the one in whose image we are made, and hence about our own vocation to be the cross-bearing people, the people in whose lives and service the living God is made known.[2]

How to Use This Book for Group Discussion

If you are using this book through Lent as part of a group study, it will be helpful for everyone to read the relevant chapter before each meeting, and then for one person to plan how the discussion and prayer will go, based upon the suggestions at the end of each chapter. Each chapter has a similar pattern, based around two continuing themes – *Reflecting on God's Word* and *Deepening our Understanding of Lent*.

Reflecting on God's Word

There is a Scripture passage in each chapter, which I suggest the group members first explore in a meditative way. Read the passage aloud once or twice, and then invite each person, one at a time, to speak a single word or phrase into the silence that follows the reading. Although it will be helpful if each person has a copy of the reading, at this point it is better if everyone just *listens* to the word, allowing themselves to connect with a particular word or phrase, rather than following it on the page. It does not matter if some people do not say a word out loud. Nor, at this point, is any explanation necessary for why someone has spoken a particular word. Just let anyone who wants to repeat back to the group the word that has struck them.

If this way of reflecting on Scripture is new to you, then you may find it takes a couple of weeks for the group to get into it. But persevere – it is a good way of listening to God's Word, based upon an ancient, monastic way of reading the Bible, known as *lectio divina* (divine reading).

Next are some discussions, which link the word or phrase people have identified with some of the chapter's themes.

Deepening our understanding of Lent

Then there are some questions on how our observation of Lent can foster our growth in faithfulness to Christ and involvement in God's mission in the world.

After this is a reading and a prayer the group can either incorporate into a time of prayer at the end of the meeting, or individuals can use after the meeting.

A Prayer for the Keeping of a Holy Lent

Lord, bless me this Lent.
Lord, let me fast most truly and profitably,
by feeding in prayer on thy Spirit:
reveal me to myself
in the light of thy holiness.
Suffer me never to think
that I have knowledge enough to need no teaching,
wisdom enough to need no correction,
talents enough to need no grace,
goodness enough to need no progress,
humility enough to need no repentance,
devotion enough to need no quickening,

strength sufficient without thy Spirit;
lest, standing still, I fall back for evermore.
Shew me the desires that should be disciplined,
and sloths to be slain.
Shew me the omissions to be made up
and the habits to be mended.
And behind these, weaken, humble and annihilate in me
self-will, self-righteousness, self-satisfaction,
self-sufficiency, self-assertion, vainglory.
May my whole effort be to return to thee;
O make it serious and sincere
persevering and fruitful in result,
by the help of thy Holy Spirit
and to thy glory,
my Lord and my God.[3]

A Prayer

Son of Man, who endured in your body
the agony of thirst in death,
and in your spirit thirsted
for the world's salvation:
deepen our understanding of your sufferings
by which our redemption was secured,
and increase in us those spiritual longings
which you alone can satisfy;
that hungering and thirsting after righteousness
we may be filled with all the fullness of God
and serve and praise you evermore.[4]

CHAPTER 1

The God Who Shares

Christ Jesus was in the form of God,
but he did not cling to equality with God.
He emptied himself, taking the form of a servant,
and was born in our human likeness.
Being found in human form, he humbled himself,
and became obedient unto death, even death on a cross;
therefore, God has highly exalted him,
and bestowed on him the name above every name,
that at the name of Jesus, every knee shall bow,
in heaven and on earth and under the earth.
And every tongue confess that Jesus Christ is Lord,
to the glory of God the Father.

PHILIPPIANS 2:5B–11[1]

In John's Gospel, just before he dies, Jesus cries out, 'I thirst' (John 19:28). The soldiers soak a sponge in sour wine and hold it up to his lips on a branch of hyssop. When Jesus has drunk the wine he bows his head and dies. 'It is finished,' he says (John 19:30).

At first glance the meaning of the words 'I thirst' is quite obvious. It is a painful and poignant moment in a grim story: Jesus is dying on the cross; he is in agony; he longs for a drink to ease his pain. What more is there to say? It is a ghastly death, made strangely more humiliating by the unnecessary indignity of the sour wine the soldiers offer.

Surely, of all Jesus' words, these cannot be stretched into a book?

But the witness of the Scriptures is that the Jesus whom we see thirsting on the cross is the one who, born in human likeness, has emptied himself of equality with God, taken the form of a servant, and become obedient even to death. 'In Christ', says St Paul, 'God was reconciling the world to himself' (2 Corinthians 5:19). This is God thirsting on the cross, sharing the world's suffering, sharing our humanity. Therefore, these words from the cross can be a window into God's purposes. As we uncover the meaning of these words we are led to a deeper appreciation of God's love for us, made known in Christ, and a deeper understanding of our own calling to follow him today.

Too many Christians rush swiftly from the agony of the passion to the blessed relief of Easter morning. Let us not repeat this mistake. Rather, let us stand beneath the cross and hear over and over again Jesus' words: 'I am thirsty,' he says to us.

The passion of God

The story is told of a mother whose little girl is late home from school one day. As the minutes tick by the mother gets more and more worried. Five minutes go by, ten minutes go by, and the mother does not know where the little girl can be. Fifteen minutes go by, twenty minutes go by and the mother starts to imagine the terrible things that may have befallen her daughter. Twenty-five minutes go by and the mother is convinced something awful has happened. Thirty minutes go by and the mother is on the verge of ringing the police. Suddenly the little girl waltzes in through the back door without a care in the world. The mother sweeps her daughter up in her arms, deeply relieved she is safe. But as is the way with parents, relief quickly turns to anger: 'Where have you been?!' the mother cries. 'Didn't you realize how worried I would be about you?'

Well, it turns out that all this while the little girl had been next door, and the woman who lives there had recently lost her husband. 'What have you been doing worrying that poor lady next door?' the mother asks, crossly.

'I haven't been worrying her,' says the little girl. 'I've been comforting her.'

'Comforting her!' retorts the mother. 'What could you possibly do to comfort her?'

The little girl replies, 'I climbed into her lap and cried with her.'

This story takes us right to the heart of what this book is about, for this is what God is like, and this is the first thing we learn about God from Jesus. In Jesus, God shares our humanity. The God revealed to us in Jesus is one who climbs into our lap and cries with us. He shares all the tremendous joys of human life. He also shares the most heart-breaking sorrows.

The supreme example of this is the crucifixion. On the cross, when Jesus cries out in thirst, the misery and anguish he is going through are not just his, though the pain is very real: they resonate with every human cry and with all human suffering. Wherever there is pain in the world, wherever someone cries out, thirsty for water, afflicted with grief, tormented by pain, or craving love, we hear the cry of the one who has come down to earth to show us what God is like. We discover that God is thirsting too. In the suffering, thirsting love of Christ we see the thirsting, suffering God.

But saying this makes an assumption many people today find extremely hard to believe, one that even many Christians doubt. What we are saying is that Jesus – the flesh and blood man from Nazareth – is also God: not just a good man who acted like a god, nor God in disguise as a man, but someone in whom the fullness of God and the fullness of humanity dwelt together. This means that what it was for Jesus to be God was contained within what it is to be human.

This truth about how God is present to us in Jesus is of vital importance for the Christian faith. If Jesus, hanging on the cross, aching with thirst, his heart broken in two, is just one more innocent man dying an ugly death, then his story has little relevance to our suffering and our dying. His example may evoke compassion, we may even marvel at his fortitude, but let's face it, there's a lot of suffering in the world, and many people have faced that suffering bravely. What difference does his death make to us? And if Jesus is not really a man at all, but some sort of superman, a god in human disguise, then again, what difference does this make to us?

But if this man – this fully human man – is also fully God, if what it is to be God and what it is to be human are joined together in this man, if in Jesus the frailty of human flesh and the eternity of God are joined together, then the story of this man's living and dying is the one upon which all the vast and important questions of life and death hang. His life and death have relevance for every life and death.

And this is the Christian claim, the Christian story. The great message of the incarnation is this – the Word that was with God in the beginning has, in Jesus, been made flesh (John 1:14). In fact, the word 'incarnation' means literally 'embodiment in flesh'. We use a form of the Latin word for flesh – *carne* (from *caro*) – unwittingly whenever we eat that popular dish *chilli con carne*, which means 'chilli with flesh'.

This is a staggering claim to make about God: that he is revealed in flesh, not overpowering what it is to be human, nor diminishing what it is to be God, but perfecting and directing humanity, and revealing God within the terms and language and particularity of a human life, the person of Jesus. Jesus shows us what God is like. Jesus also makes God available to us.

This making God known through Jesus is a central teaching of the New Testament. Paul, in his letter to the Colossians, says that Jesus is the 'image of the invisible God' (Colossians 1:15) and 'in him the fullness of God was pleased to dwell' (Colossians 1:19). In him 'we have access to God,' says the letter to the Ephesians (Ephesians 3:12).

In John's Gospel, Jesus himself says, when Philip idly asks him to show them the Father, 'Have I been with you all this time, Philip, and you still do not know me? Whoever has seen me has seen the Father . . . Believe me that I am in the Father and the Father is in me' (John 14:9,11). Therefore, if we want to know what God is like, we must look at Jesus. Jesus is God's way of knowing God. And what we find in Jesus is a God who knows what it is like to be human.

A thousand sentimental Christmas cards have blunted the edge of the Christian faith's radical message. We see the cosy scene – a child lying in a bed of warm straw, adoring parents, angels, shepherds – and we miss the essential offensiveness of the story. This is not how we expect God to be. This is not a God who is above and beyond us, but a very 'come down to earth' God. This is not the comforting image of an almighty God, but of a God who chooses to reveal himself as stripped of power, a God who identifies himself with human beings – an affront to the usual religious mindset that likes to keep God's sacredness separate from the supposed profanity of flesh. And what do we hear God saying to us? Well, the first utterance of the newborn is a cry, and the first thirsting of the newborn is for his mother's milk. In Jesus, God cries out to us; he is thirsty. And in the manger we find a God who shares all it means to be human. In the manger is a God who thirsts. This was the experience of God in Jesus. He is born as one of us: his thirst is quenched at his mother's breast, and he knows the intimacy and comfort of his mother's love. What the Christian story reveals to us is what we can really only call the *weakness* of God. He is still God, still the all-powerful creator and sustainer of the universe, but no longer unapproachable, distant and removed. Rather, in Bethlehem, we find him very close and in need of help, a weak and fragile God, one who has become a tiny, helpless child, one who has made himself dependent on us. He is crying in the manger and requires our service. He is nailed to a cross and cries out for a drink. He chooses to express his sovereignty and all-powerfulness through the frailty of human flesh.

Thus we can affirm that Jesus' death is not just one more innocent waste of life, but in Jesus, God *shares* human life. The one who died on the cross, crying out in thirst, is the one who was born in the manger, the one who shares. By sharing our life on earth he makes it possible for us to share his life in heaven. Because he shared our humanity we can share his divinity. In Augustine's famous phrase, 'he becomes what we are, in order that we might become what he is'.

The Athanasian Creed puts it like this:

> Although he is both divine and human
> He is not two beings but one Christ.
> One, not by turning God into flesh,
> but by taking humanity into God.[2]

Emmanuel

At his birth, Jesus receives two names, both of which have great meaning. First, he is called Jesus, which means, literally, 'God rescues'. Jesus is the one who is coming to save people. But he is also called Emmanuel, which means 'God is with us'.

The one whom we see as a helpless child is God with us. The one whom we see impaled on the cross is also God with us. Because of him our whole understanding of God, and of God's involvement with the world, is completely changed. His life and death reveal the true nature of God as the one who shares, as the one who communicates his complete and self-surrendering regard for his creation by becoming part of it, by becoming the one who is with us, who has climbed into our lap and holds us, weeping with us, dying with us. In Jesus, God speaks to us in a language we can understand, the language of a human life.

From this point onwards we can no longer think of God as one who is unaware of our human predicament or uninterested in our plight. He is right alongside us, holding our hand when the pain is at its worst and leading the way, the only glimmer of light when everything else is lost and dark.

And his purpose is love. God becomes flesh in Jesus in order to love in the only way love knows how: to offer love without any thought of reward, and without any hint of compulsion that we should love in return. What we see here in the thirsting of Jesus, first at his birth, and then in his passion and death, is his sharing our humanity – sharing it to offer love, and sharing it to communicate love in a loving way.

Thus a pattern is set for the whole of Jesus' life and ministry. He walks the path of love; he never coerces or manipulates. The prophet Isaiah puts it like this:

> a bruised reed he will not break,
> and a dimly burning wick he will not quench. (Isaiah 42:3)

As we shall see later, these are words that in all probability Jesus himself contemplated deeply to understand his own vocation. Jesus doesn't just show us love; he isn't just loving; he is love, because he is God, sharing our humanity, drawing us to himself and through him to the Father, and doing this all by love.

John baptizes Jesus in the river Jordan, not because he needs baptism (after all, he is the one person who does not require forgiveness!) but because his mission is to show complete solidarity with his beloved. He heals the sick, he forgives those trapped in sin, he restores the outcast to life in the community, he feeds the hungry, and he speaks words of hope and challenge. He shows us a new way of living. He demonstrates a glorious and liberating humanity. He brings God down to earth, and takes earth up to God.

But at the human level there is also, whatever the particular circumstances of his death might be, the stark and simple truth that to share human living to the full must also mean sharing death. And when it comes to finding solace amid all the deaths and sufferings of human life, it is here, more than anywhere, that we see what being Emmanuel really means.

The way of the cross

Jesus knew that his vocation, to be the one who shares and rescues, would bring him into conflict with the religious authorities of his day. He often spoke to his disciples of his impending death and tried to prepare them for what would happen afterwards, and what it would mean for their lives (though they barely understood a word of what he was saying).

He tried to evade the snares set for him by the Jewish religious authorities, but in the end there was no place to turn. To be true to his vocation meant also to challenge the authorities. While claiming to speak for God, they were actually getting in the way of this new and complete revelation of God's purpose and nature. Jesus saw clearly that those authorities were chiefly concerned with preserving their own power and status, but in doing so were cutting themselves off from God. The tragic irony is that all this was done in the name of God: upright, law-abiding religious people arrested and executed Jesus!

But religion can be dangerous. There is always the tendency to replace the risky freedom of relationship with God with the controlling safety of a religious system, where some are counted in while others are excluded, and where rules and regulations monitor and control belief as well as behaviour.

It might be going a bit far to say that Jesus came to do away with religion. Certainly it seems doubtful that he ever intended to start a new one. He came to fulfil the religion that was Judaism (and in a sense, therefore, *all* religion) by drawing together in himself the longing of religious faith, the hopes of the human spirit, and the searching, saving love of God.

Of course, there is now a religion that bears Jesus Christ's name – Christianity. Like other religions it has its rules and systems, which often make it unattractive to people today. But the Christian faith is first and foremost about a person – Jesus, the revelation of God – who leads us into community with God. Christianity is thus a way of living, and Christians live as followers of Jesus, finding purpose and value to life in and through him.

And this was what so infuriated and confounded the religious people of Jesus' day, as it continues to infuriate and confound today. Jesus' claim to speak and act directly with the authority of God is not a claim about which we can remain indifferent. Either it is true, or it is dangerous and blasphemous nonsense.

The tragedy of God's mission of love to the world in Jesus (but the risk God was prepared to take, such is love's nature) was that the Messiah would go unrecognized, that he would be rejected and eliminated. Jesus saw that this would happen, and when he started to challenge the authority of the temple itself (overturning the moneylenders' tables and claiming to rebuild the temple in three days) events began moving quickly.

Such a threat to the establishment and power of the Jewish faith had to be dealt with swiftly and completely. There was no room for mercy. Jesus' brief ministry of teaching and healing came to an abrupt end in Jerusalem when those arresting him handed him over to the religious authorities and then to the Roman occupying forces, who would carry out the death sentence.

His final journey from the governor's palace, where he was condemned to death by crucifixion, to Golgotha ('the place of the skull') outside the city walls, was a journey of about 640 metres (700 yards). Carrying his own cross and dressed up as a puppet king, he was led out to die. We will look at the terrible details of crucifixion in a later chapter, but suffice to say here, it was a ghastly, long drawn out and painful way of dying.

The appalling suffering of Jesus is captured in his words 'I thirst.' Some of the words of Jesus are difficult to understand, and require scholarly interpretation, but these are plain and very human. They take us to the heart of God, for in the passion and death of Jesus, God demonstrates his complete identification with us. They take us to the heart of pain, because although we may not have used these actual words, we too have often uttered cries of anguish in the sufferings we have experienced.

On the cross Jesus cries out in torment. His throat is dry and his tongue cleaves to his jaws as he tries to suck the last few drops of moisture from his mouth. He thirsts, like those whose pictures we have seen on our television screens, the many broken, hungry people crying out. All around the world people are starving and millions are dying for lack of clean water. He shares that terrible thirst. When we see their faces we see the face of Christ.

Some of us have seen the end of our dying loved ones, as we sit by their beds and offer a damp flannel to their lips, or give them a sip of water. Jesus shares their final moments. He shares our love for them.

But as we watch our television screens and see awful images of devastation and need, and as we minister to our loved ones as they die, bigger questions confront us. Even if we do recognize the presence of Christ in these sufferings, we still cry out to God in anguish, 'Why does all this happen?'

Making sense of pain

When I was 20, Lawrence, a close friend of mine, died. He was a pilot in the Royal Air Force and his plane crashed somewhere over the sea near Scotland. His body was never recovered. One day he was alive and well with his whole life in front of him. The next day he was gone. It all seemed tragic and pointless. I remember sitting in the church during the funeral service, half comforted by the confident ceremonies that accompany Christian dying, and half despairing – how could the random meaninglessness of his death be squared with belief in a God of order and justice and love? There didn't seem to be a match.

That was the first time I discovered how fickle death could be. Looking back, I was probably fortunate to have avoided such a personal brush with death for so long. Relatives of mine had died, and I had mourned their passing, but it had always seemed like they had had their allotted three score years and ten: they seemed old and ready for death, so there seemed no injustice involved. But when Lawrence died I wanted to rage against a universe that could be so cruel as to swallow into nothingness, in the twinkling of an eye, a life that had barely begun.

And, of course, the death of Lawrence is just one death in a catalogue of suffering too immense to survey. I am writing this 23 years later and only yesterday I learned of the death of another old friend, Jane, a girl I knew when I was at school. Earlier this year she contracted cancer of the liver. She deteriorated quickly and died, leaving behind two young children, who now have to grow up without their mother.

And in between the deaths of Lawrence and Jane have been many other deaths and much innocent suffering.

I am the same age as the few survivors from Aberfan in Wales. I was seven when that disaster happened: a slagheap slipped on to a school and killed hundreds of children. It was my first warning that the world was not the safe place I had thought it to be. I now began to realize that it could be wild, unpredictable and deadly.

My eldest son is the same age Jamie Bulger would be, were he still alive. Jamie, a toddler, was kidnapped in 1993 in Liverpool by two older boys, themselves only ten and eleven, and killed. My son is also the age the children killed in Dunblane Primary School in Scotland in 1996 would be, had they not died. In that incident 17 children and a teacher were shot by a deranged gunman. Those of you in other parts of the world will already have remembered the horrors and tragedies that have happened in your own country. All this suffering is appalling, but is worse when children are involved. It is not just the crime itself that appals, but the destruction of innocence, the loss of hope. And with a horrible and grim irony I find myself sitting and writing this as another tragedy unfolds. This week someone discovered the bodies of the missing schoolgirls Holly Wells and Jessica Chapman who came from a village near Cambridge. It now seems likely that the person who abducted and murdered them (and heaven knows what else) was someone they knew and trusted. People reading this book in Britain will be familiar with these incidents: they are etched into our collective consciousness.

With each of these tragedies I have done what I imagine most parents do: I hug my children tightly, wanting to protect them from the random evil and caprice that stalks our world, but also knowing my powers are very limited. Whether I like it or not, this universe we inhabit is full of danger.

Each of us carries through life the names of those we love who have lost their lives, or who have been the victims of terrible suffering. They are our own litany of horror, reminding us of the fragility of life, but sometimes driving us to question whether there is any ultimate truth or purpose at all. Indeed, many people outside the Christian community consider the existence of cancer and earthquakes and droughts, let alone the horrors wrought by human cruelty, sufficient to render all belief in God utter stupidity. All of us recall the bloody awfulness of the Somme, Auschwitz and Hiroshima, which together blew away the optimism of several generations in the last century. But with the fall of the Berlin Wall, and despite many other conflicts across the world, we dared to believe again that the future could be better than the past. All that now seems fragile. The terror of 11 September 2001 is seared on to our memory. With the crumbling of the Twin Towers of the World Trade Center so much of our hope for a new millennium also dwindled away. The world seems more frightening than ever.

In such a situation we Christians ask ourselves (and are asked by others) why the world is this way. Or, more precisely, why did God make it this way? Why does God allow this outrageous suffering? How can a God who is supposed to be generous and loving permit the ghastly injustices and indignities that are the daily lot of this broken yet beautiful world? Where can we go to make sense of all this pain?

In Peterborough Cathedral, where I serve, these painful questions have been given voice in the prayers left by visitors to the cathedral and in the things people have written in the books of condolence for Holly Wells and Jessica Chapman. 'God, where were you when Holly and Jessica needed you?' is the question in a child's handwriting stuck up on our intercession board. 'How can there be a God when children are made to suffer?' asks another.

When faced with these questions, what can we Christians say in God's defence? First, we have to be honest and acknowledge that we do not have a satisfactory answer to this most basic of questions, and probably never will. But if we were to imagine a situation where we were able to address God directly, and accuse him of being uncaring and fickle, what would his defence be? What would he say to us?

Surely there would be only one word. And that word would be Jesus, God's Word made flesh. Jesus alone is God's defence against the accusations of cruelty and indifference, though the word 'defence' seems inappropriate in this context. If we were to bring God to court, and have him stand condemned as a cruel and heartless God, the first and only witness he would call in his defence is also the one who bears upon his body the incriminating evidence amassed by the prosecution: the wounds of Jesus' passion are both the sign of God's involvement in the world and the most vivid marks of the world's suffering. The case would be dismissed. The one who stands condemned in the dock cannot be the perpetrator of the crime, for he is also its victim. This revelation of God's involvement has not made the suffering any less. Nor has it told us why the world should be this way. All we know is that God is involved in it – neither causing it, nor indifferent to it. In Jesus he has plumbed the depths of pain. He knows what it's like to be human. As the writer of the letter to the Hebrews puts it, 'For we do not have a high priest who is unable to sympathize with our weaknesses, but we have one who in every respect has been tested as we are, yet without sin. Let us therefore approach the throne of grace with boldness, so that we may receive mercy and find grace to help in time of need' (Hebrews 4:15–16).

Responding to pain

Jesus also shows us how to respond to suffering and pain. He shows us how we contribute to the pain and suffering of the world, and he shows us how we can alleviate that suffering. He shows us not only the immense power of God's love, but also its limits.

Love can only be love. If, as the Scriptures claim, God is love (1 John 4:16) – not just very loving, but love itself – he can only do what love can do. The self-emptying of his power to become a human being is a demonstration of this love. Our freedom to choose how we live, and how we respond to what happens to us, is a prerequisite for being able to love. It is what we mean when we say we are made in the image of God. We are made by the one who is love. We are given the capacity to love. We therefore have the terrible, risky gift of freedom.

Put plainly, if we were not free we could not love. We might have affection or even loyalty; but we would have these things because we had no choice. To be love, it has to be free.

If the creation of the universe is an act of self-forgetful love that spends all to make possible a world where love can be both received and returned, there is the risk that love will be spurned. This accounts for our terrible misuse of human freedom when we plunder the earth's natural resources, the appalling disparities between rich and poor, the greed and lust that builds empires and exploits multitudes. God's love thus carries with it the potential for sin and bears the bitter harvest of warfare, discontent, starvation and death.

Can it also account for a universe that contains HIV, cancer and earthquakes? We do not know, for we are at the very limits of human knowledge. But if we know that the good fruits of love can flourish only where there is freedom, and that this must carry with it the possibility of love's shadow – sin and hate – prevailing, then perhaps it is at least reasonable to see this as a way of making sense of pain.

At the heart of it all rests the revelation of God in Jesus Christ. Through Jesus we come to know the God who shares. Through Jesus we come to know the God who loves. Where can we go to make sense of the suffering of the world? Ultimately, there is only one place: the cross of Jesus Christ.

The story of the cross – the terrible story of one who is falsely accused, abandoned by his friends, stripped and humiliated, who cries out in pain, who experiences desolation and loss, who dies a ghastly death, parched and thirsty – is also the beautiful story of the God who comes to earth to share our humanity, who dies to share our dying, and who rises again to show us death is not the end and to create a new communion between earth and heaven. It is a story where we discover how completely God shares what it is to be human. It is a story where we discover how completely God loves. This is a completely unexpected God: not all-powerful, but self-emptying and self-sacrificing; not in control, but handed over. It is the story of Love.

Only by exploring the remarkable love of this nailed-to-a-cross God can we begin to understand our own mortality and suffering. Only by following him can we become the people we long to be, achieve the fulfilment we crave, discover our full potential as his sons and daughters.

Implications for Today

Many implications arise when we consider Jesus' words 'I thirst' as a sign of God's sharing in the suffering of the world. I want to look at two in particular: (1) how we face pain and death, and (2) how we discover balance, and therefore fulfilment, in our life.

The first of these is a vital issue for our culture. We are adept at avoiding all talk of death, and much of our culture's emphasis on youth and beauty is a denial of our mortality, so that we end up seeing death as an embarrassing personal failure. It is to human ingenuity and the marketplace that we look for help. The ultimate 'must-have' purchase for many is a new face, or a new body – anything to stave off the effects of ageing and to cheat death. But Christ's passion opens up to us new ways of seeing and understanding human frailty.

The second implication – restoring balance in our lives – will lead us to explore the first of six Lenten disciplines we will look at through the book, namely fasting. The Christian fast is one of the best antidotes to consumerism. It leads us to embrace reality, especially our mortality and dependence on God.

Facing pain and death

Let us state the situation in a rather basic way: pain is painful. Believing in the death and resurrection of Jesus Christ, and believing that ultimately victory will swallow up all death and all pain, does not make the pain I am experiencing now any less painful. Nor does it take away the fear of pain and death.

The ghastly experience of suffering is always isolating and dispiriting. We may well see it in a different way – through the lens of Christ's passion – and this may help us in our times of trial, but it will not help us when we are faced with the sufferings of those around us, who look to us for help. At these times we need to be Emmanuel people who express Christ's love through our presence alongside those in pain. We don't pretend we know what they are going through, but we commit ourselves to being with them in the midst of their torment.

There is also a certain grim solidarity in suffering – it comes to us all one way or another. But each person suffers in her or his own particular way. There may be others worse off than you (I for one have never found this thought particularly comforting), but even if their suffering is worse than yours, it does not take your pain away.

Neither should we pretend we have all the answers. We do not point people to Christ with our words; we *become* Christ by our deeds. We *offer* the love, the compassion, the mercy and the understanding of Christ by the way we stick with people in their times of difficulty and suffering. We mediate Christ's love.

Too often today we avoid one another's pain. When meeting someone who is bereaved we fail to mention the person who has died. We act as if nothing has changed. When pushed to say something at all, we offer the platitude that time is a great healer. But often time does not heal. When meeting a terminally ill person we talk about anything and everything except impending death. And if we mention that person's illness, we talk optimistically about recovery and admire that person's bravery in the face of ill health's adversity, as if valour ever postponed death!

Even Christians are prone to this unreality in the face of death. Before I was ordained I worked at St Christopher's Hospice for the dying for a year. The saddest sight I saw there was earnest Christians praying around the deathbed of their father, who had only hours to live, and calling upon God to save him. God was saving him, but not in the way their prayers were imploring. His healing was to be a gracious letting go of this life. But those around him could not face this truth.

The way of Christ is a way that acknowledges the reality of pain, that looks it in the eye. It embraces pain, not because pain is good, nor because it can be made any less painful by being embraced, but because this is the way the world is. The journey of our life must pass through the way of suffering and death, and we all experience this in different ways. Some have to bear a heavy burden of suffering, enduring one illness after another for many years; others have their lives unjustly, and swiftly, cut short. Others enjoy what we call good health and live for many years. Nevertheless, it is still true, indeed it is the deepest truth of all, that this life, this way of pain and joy, is a journey home to God. In the end there is a 'deathday' for each of us, just like there is a birthday. On that day the greatest prayer of healing we can utter is not that our life on earth is restored to us, but that we might let go of this life and cleave to God.

In John's Gospel, after Jesus has cried out on the cross, 'I thirst,' he says, 'It is finished' (John 19:30), which kind of means, 'It is over; it is complete'. He is able to let go of life; he has done what he came to do.

In Luke's account of the passion this point is made with even greater clarity. Quoting Psalm 31, Jesus says as he dies, 'Father, into your hands I commend my spirit' (Luke 23:46).

In today's church we need a more robust openness when it comes to talking about death. Death is the reality that shapes our life and we need to prepare well for it. The greatest experiences I had in St Christopher's Hospice were when Christian men and women embraced dying with trust and openness. In my subsequent ministry as a priest in the church it has always been intensely moving to minister to those who are close to death and who are able to look death in the eye. I remember a lady in my parish in Chichester who insisted on dying in the living room. She didn't want to be stuck away in an upstairs bedroom. She wanted to die as she had lived, with family and friends around her, and getting on with life as best she could. So a bed was made up for her in the living room, and she did indeed live until the day it came for her to die.

More recently, here in Peterborough, I received a phone call one Sunday afternoon. A very old lady, housebound for many years and now close to death, requested that a priest come and pray with her and give her the last rites. She wanted a priest from the cathedral, because that was where she had worshipped when she had been able to get to church. (Some people think that priests are often called to people's deathbeds, but in my experience this is something that happens infrequently.)

This was a beautiful experience. Her family was gathered around her in the dishevelled front room of her little house. We all prayed together, and although she couldn't join in she was conscious of what was happening around her. I anointed her and said the lovely prayer for the dying, which begins, 'Go forth on your journey from this world . . .'[3] I chatted with the family and left. A few hours later they phoned me again to say that she had died. And this in turn reminds me of another person, a man who came to faith during the last weeks of a very painful terminal illness. He was due to be confirmed and receive his first Holy Communion, when he took a severe turn for the worse. It was reckoned that he would die within 24 hours. No bishop could be found to confirm at such short notice and I was given special permission to perform the rite. I heard his confession, confirmed him and gave him Holy Communion. Within an hour of receiving the sacraments he slipped into unconsciousness and died. His last words were the amens of his prayers.

Christians of a previous generation would have described these experiences as 'happy deaths'. Indeed, it is not so long ago that Christians used to pray for a happy death. But now we prefer not to think about it at all. The season of Lent, however, allows us no such denial. Ash Wednesday plunges us (very nearly drowns us!) in the deep waters of death.

In many churches a ceremony takes place on Ash Wednesday where we are marked on our foreheads with the sign of the cross, with the burnt ashes of the previous year's palm crosses. This is a sign that the promise of glory that heralded Jesus' entry into Jerusalem turned quickly to despair. Jesus will be victorious, but not in a way anyone has imagined. With this bleak and sobering ceremony the season of Lent begins.

It is this ceremony that gives Ash Wednesday its name. Through it we are brought face to face with the reality of Christ's death; and only through his death will we find the promise of his resurrection. In order to be real about the death of Christ we need to be real about ourselves, our own mortality and our own sinfulness. So often we live our lives as if we will enjoy good health indefinitely, and as if life on earth goes on forever. We expend huge amounts of time, money and energy trying to postpone death, or at least cover up any signs of its approach. We inhabit a kind of fantasy world, a virtual reality, where the right amount of exercise, a high-fibre diet, and the odd medical intervention will somehow keep us immune from suffering, and enable us to live forever. We know that this isn't actually the case, but we live in a permanent state of denial, an alternative universe, so that when suffering and death do come, even at the end of a long life, we greet them as unexpected intruders rather than as friends to lead us home. Consequently, we have lost most of the rituals that accompanied dying. We just don't know how to die anymore, and we push death into a corner. You see this in many hospitals, the dying still left at the end of the ward, with the curtains round the bed.

Ash Wednesday brings us up short. As the ashes are traced on our foreheads the priest says these words: 'Remember that you are dust, and to dust you shall return.'[4] If you come to church looking for good cheer this doesn't sound like what you had in mind. This, surely, isn't the good news the gospel speaks about? Yet this is precisely the best news of all, because this is the proclamation of reality. We are all going to die. This is the basic fact of our life, the destination towards which all our lives are travelling, the reality that frames our life. Unless we acknowledge it, we will never have the grace to stand at the foot of the cross and discover the reality of God's involvement with our life – still less the liberating challenge of God's love and forgiveness. Lent is thus an invitation to embrace reality.

Restoring balance: fasting and self-denial

There isn't much knowledge of the Christian tradition left in our culture, but ask someone what they know about Lent, and they will probably tell you it is a time to give things up, particularly things pleasurable. And to an extent they are right. Lent is the Christian fast, though very few Christians treat it in this way today, as fasting and self-denial are not overpopular in a society pledged to pursuing material well-being and hedonistic self-fulfilment!

But the Christian story tells us that the way to life passes through the way of the cross, that true self-fulfilment can only be found by proper self-denial. This does not mean hating yourself, or putting yourself down, or seeking hardship and discomfort: it means finding balance in life.

I heard on the radio recently about a man who eats Christmas dinner every day. Every day he pulls a cracker with himself, puts on his paper hat and sits down to roast turkey with stuffing, Christmas pudding to follow – the full works. An oddball? Yes. An eccentric? Most certainly. But is he really that different from the rest of us? Most of us want and indeed expect all the good things life has to offer. We want them now, and we want them by right, giving little thought to the effect of our behaviour on those around us, or on the rest of the planet, and paying scant attention to the effects of this imbalance on our spiritual lives.

We pursue lives of excess and indulgence. We want to get to places fast, so we drive our cars faster. This leads to more accidents on the roads, more stress, and more congestion. But did you know that driving at 50 miles (80 kilometres) per hour uses 25 per cent less fuel than driving at 70 miles (113 kilometres) per hour. And what if we shared our car, or got on the bus or got on our bikes?

We like eating strawberries in winter, or we have developed a taste for other exotic vegetables, so we abandon locally grown produce, or the fruits of each season, so that we can eat what we want to when we want to. And, in so doing, we often end up exploiting and disrupting the developing-world economies where these foods are grown, wasting precious and finite resources in having them transported to our doorsteps.

I could easily cite more examples of the debilitating environmental effects of a globalized economy. But let us focus here for a moment on the spiritual effects. When every day is a day of plenty and of celebration, there is nothing left to look forward to. When every day is Christmas day, Christmas day is lost forever.

Fasting and self-denial are not about denying life: on the contrary, in providing a balance to life they lead the way to true celebration. Without a fast there can never be a feast.

In order to find your true self, you need to let go of yourself. Jesus says, 'If any want to become my followers, let them deny themselves and take up their cross and follow me. For those who want to save their lives will lose it, and those who lose their life for my sake will find it. For what will it profit them if they gain the whole world but forfeit their life?' (Matthew 16:24–26a).

Therefore, consider practising the discipline of the fast this Lent. I don't mean just giving up ice cream or dough-nuts. The object of the Christian fast is to deny ourselves something normally experienced as fundamental to life, so that we grow in our appreciation that all things come from God and that without God there is nothing. Hence, we return to the thing we have missed, with a real thanksgiv-ing and a much fuller enjoyment.

In which case, consider giving up a whole meal once a week. Or give up coffee or alcohol. Or give up your daily newspaper or television. Or give up driving your car so fast, or driving it so often. You can give the time saved to God in a more profound thanksgiving for the whole of life. You can give the money saved to those in need as a small token of your desire to build a fairer world. Thus your acts of fasting and self-denial, however small, will begin to draw you into the mystery of the one who gave up everything for you.

In the Sermon on the Mount, Jesus has some things to say about fasting. He begins by saying, '*Whenever* you fast . . .' (Matthew 6:16; my emphasis). In other words, he is taking it for granted that you will fast, not suggesting it as something you may not have thought of. He goes on, 'do not look dismal, like the hypocrites', but when you fast, let it be 'seen not by others but by your Father who is in secret' (Matthew 6:18). Fasting is not supposed to be a signal to others of our own spiritual seriousness, but is a way of deep-ening our relationship with God by leading us to a deeper appreciation of God's goodness to us in the many ways he provides for us. Fasting is a secret joy.

Though he was in the form of God, Jesus did not cling to equality with God, but emptied himself, taking the form of a servant, and was born in our human likeness. He thirsted on the cross as a sign of his involvement in our life. Now he invites us to be involved in his life. In this way we can find the fulfilment we long for. The paradox of the Christian faith is that it is a fulfilment found by subduing our own desires. Through acts of self-denial we discover the primacy, the beauty, the generosity and the dependability of God: everything comes from him. By fasting we discover within ourselves a thirst for God: we long for a new intimacy with God in our prayer and a renewed adoration in our worship. By experiencing a little of the privations so many suffer through no fault of their own we discover a new longing for God's ways to be known on earth, a righteous indignation and a desire for justice. We are put back in touch with basic realities about our own mortality, about the way our life is sustained, about our solidarity with our fellow human beings. This is the balance our lives require. Left out of kilter we easily self-destruct.

A Final Thought

Without God there is nothing. Or perhaps we would better say of our society, without God there is everything, but it loses its value, it fails to satisfy. We gorge ourselves more and more on what the world has to offer, but it does not quench our thirst.

Letting go of this, learning to put it in its place as secondary to God, not only restores balance to our lives, but actually helps us to enjoy the good things of the world even more.

For Discussion

Reflecting on God's Word

1 Read either Philippians 2:5–11 *or* Colossians 1:15–20.

2 Spend some time in silence.

3 Invite people to speak aloud into the silence a word or phrase that strikes them from the passage.

4 In pairs or small groups share with each other the words and phrases that have been spoken and how they shed light on our own experiences and response to suffering. Has it made any discernible difference in our own lives to know that God shares our suffering in Christ?

Deepening our understanding of Lent

1 How does thinking about Christ's death help us to feel about our own death? Have we in any sense prepared ourselves for death? And what does this mean, anyway?

2 How might fasting help us to experience the sovereignty of God?

3 How might fasting put us back in touch with some basic realities about life?

4 Are there some simple, practical ways we can fast during this Lent, and monitor together in this group what difference it makes?

For Reflection

And the words of Christ dying came to mind, 'I thirst'. I saw that he was thirsty in a twofold sense, physical and spiritual – of this latter I shall be speaking later. The immediate purpose of this particular word was to stress the physical thirst, which I assumed to be caused by drying up of the moisture. For that blessed flesh and frame was drained of all blood and moisture. Because of the pull of the nails and the weight of that blessed body it was a long time. For I could see that the great, hard, hurtful nails in those dear and tender hands and feet caused the wounds to gape wide and the body to sag forward under its own weight, and because of the time it hung there. His head was scarred and torn, and the crown was sticking to it, congealed with blood; his dear hair and his withered flesh was entangled with the thorns, and they with it. At first, when the flesh was still fresh and bleeding the constant pressure of the thorns made the wounds even deeper. Furthermore, I could see that the dear skin and tender flesh, the hair and the blood, were hanging loose from the bone, gouged by the thorns in many places. It seemed about to drop off, heavy and loose, still holding its natural moisture, sagging like a cloth. The sight caused me dreadful and great grief; I would have died rather than see it fall off. What the cause of it was I could not see, but I assumed it was due to the sharp thorns, and the rough and cruel way the garland was pressed home heartlessly and pitilessly. All this continued awhile, and then it began to change before my very eyes, and I marvelled. I saw that it was beginning to dry, and therefore to lose weight, and to congeal around the garland. And as it went right round the head, it made another garland under the first. The garland of thorns was dyed the colour of his blood, and this second garland of blood, and his head generally, were the colour of blood that is congealed and dry. What could be seen of the skin of his face was covered with tiny wrinkles, and was tan coloured; it was like a plank when it has been planed and dried out. The face was browner than the body.

The cause of this dryness was fourfold: the first was caused by his bloodlessness; the second by the ensuing pain; the third by his hanging in the air, like some cloth hung out to dry; the fourth was due to his physical need of drink – and there was no comfort to relieve all his suffering and discomfort. Hard and grievous pain![5]

> Thou art indeed just, Lord, if I contend
> With thee; but, sir, so what I plead is just.
> Why do sinners' ways prosper? and why must
> Disappointment all I endeavoured end?
> Wert thou my enemy, O thou my friend,
> How wouldst thou worse, I wonder, than thou dost
> Defeat, thwart me? Oh, the sots and thralls of lust
> Do in spare hours more thrive than I that spend,
> Sir, life upon thy cause. See, banks and brakes
> Now, leaved how thick! laced they are again
> With fretty chervil, look, and fresh wind shakes
> Them; birds build – but not I build; no, but strain,
> Time's eunuch, and not breed one work that wakes.
> Mine, O thou lord of life, send my roots rain.[6]

For Prayer

Christ, I see thy crown of thorns in every eye, thy bleeding, wounded naked body in every soul; thy death liveth in every memory; thy wounded body is embalmed in every affection; thy pierced feet are bathed in everyone's tears; and it is my privilege to enter with thee into every soul.[7]

CHAPTER 2

The Word That Shapes

Answer me, O LORD, for your steadfast love is good;
according to your abundant mercy, turn to me.
Do not hide your face from your servant,
for I am in distress — make haste to answer me.
Draw near to me, redeem me,
set me free because of my enemies.
You know the insults I receive,
and my shame and dishonour;
my foes are all known to you.
Insults have broken my heart,
so that I am in despair.
I looked for pity, but there was none;
and for comforters, but I found none.
They gave me poison for food,
and for my thirst they gave me vinegar to drink.

PSALM 69:16–21

According to St John, Jesus says, 'I thirst', in order to fulfil Scripture. The passage John probably has in mind is from Psalm 69 (v. 21):

They gave me poison for food,
and for my thirst they gave me vinegar to drink.

Or perhaps he was thinking of Psalm 22, which begins, 'My God, my God why have you forsaken me?', the psalm that, according to Matthew 27:46 and Mark 15:34, Jesus quotes as he cries out in anguish.

Further on the same psalm says:

> I am poured out like water,
> and all my bones are out of joint;
> my heart is like wax;
> it is melted within my breast;
> my mouth is dried up like a potsherd,
> and my tongue sticks to my jaws;
> you lay me in the dust of death. (Psalm 22:14–15)

I thirst, I am dying of thirst, the psalmist seems to be saying.

Indeed, both of these psalms, when read in the light of the crucifixion, seem to be a commentary upon the drama of the cross. It is in Psalm 22 that we find the words 'I can count all of my bones' (Psalm 22:17): words John alludes to later in his passion narrative when he goes to some lengths to explain that not one of Jesus' bones are broken; this is 'so that the scripture might be fulfilled' (John 19:36).

This is also the psalm where it says in the next verse, 'they divide my clothes among themselves, / and for my clothing they cast lots' (Psalm 22:18), an incident all the Gospel writers mention. Indeed, a footnote in some Bibles tells us that in some ancient versions of Matthew's Gospel, after the soldiers have divided Jesus' clothes among themselves by casting lots, it says that this happened 'in order that what had been spoken through the prophet might be fulfilled'.

But John does not mention these details because it seems to him (as it may seem to us) a series of fascinating coincidences; rather, he addresses an issue of great concern for the early church: the relationship between the revelation of God in Jesus, and the revelation of God through the Law and the Prophets, what we now call the Old Testament. The first Christians believed Jesus was the Messiah, the one Israel's history and Scriptures looked forward to. We tend to think of the word 'Christ' as if it is Jesus' surname. But it is, of course, a messianic title, 'the anointed one'. And the fact that it becomes linked with Jesus from such an early date shows how crucial it is to an understanding of who he is, and what his ministry means. But there are some stark questions to ask. Why, if Jesus was God's Messiah, did he suffer such a humiliating death? Why did the Jewish religious leaders reject him? Why were they persecuting the church? These were the questions Jesus' first followers had to face, questions that lie behind much of the New Testament. In looking at them here we will begin to understand what it means for Jesus' death and resurrection to be described as happening 'according to scripture'. After all, the first followers of Jesus were all good, faithful Jews. Their concern was to make sense of the dramatic events of Jesus' death and resurrection. Later on, as the early church split with Judaism and faced even greater persecution, the integrity and intelligibility of the gospel itself depended upon their being able to make a coherent case that Jesus, the crucified one, was indeed God's Messiah, 'a stumbling-block to Jews and foolishness to Gentiles, but to those who are the called, both Jews and Greeks, Christ the power of God and the wisdom of God' (1 Corinthians 1:23–24).

Christ: the fulfilment of Scripture

The consistent claim of the early church is that all this – the rejection of the Messiah, the formation of a new Israel, the opening up of God's plan for all people, the passion, death and resurrection of Jesus – happened to *fulfil* Scripture. This is strong language. What is being claimed is a thrust and purpose in the writings of the Old Testament that leads naturally and unswervingly to the particular revelation of God that is his Son Jesus Christ – what we call the New Testament. Indeed, Jesus himself had said in the Sermon on the Mount, 'Do not think that I have come to abolish the law or the prophets; I have come not to abolish but to fulfil' (Matthew 5:17).

We must also remember that many Jewish scholars and leaders disagreed with (and still disagree with!) this interpretation. Their reading of Scripture led them to very different expectations about the coming of the Messiah.

Most prophecies about the Messiah were about a coming king. As we have said, the very words 'Messiah' and 'Christ' mean in the Hebrew and Greek languages 'the anointed one'. It is kings who are anointed at their coronation, and the Jewish religious leaders simply did not recognize Jesus as their king. They believed his claims were blasphemous and his death on the cross conclusive proof of his failure – his crucifixion was ample evidence that God had rejected him. Therefore, he couldn't be the Messiah. Rather, he was just another false messiah, an impostor.

We are so used to thinking of the cross as Christ's victory that it is hard for us to get inside the mind of those who would see it as a failure. However, if you are expecting a messiah who will come to restore your national fortunes, someone like King David, who will kick out the Romans and re-establish the political kingdom and autonomy of Israel, then dying on a cross at the hands of those you are supposed to overthrow is not a good start. It wasn't that people weren't expecting a messiah; they just weren't expecting one like Jesus! They were expecting (indeed, they believed their Scriptures *prepared* them to expect) someone different.

But, of course, the first followers of Jesus had themselves taken a long time to realize that Jesus was God's Messiah. They had different expectations of what the Messiah would be like. They also weren't expecting someone like Jesus, and it is only very slowly that the truth dawns upon them; and even then it takes a long while for it to sink in, let alone make a difference in their lives. Only the resurrection really validates the claims of Jesus' messiahship.

There is a famous passage in each of the Synoptic Gospels (Matthew, Mark and Luke's Gospels are called 'the Synoptics' because they all share the same basic synopsis of the story) where Peter at last recognizes who Jesus is (Matthew 16:13–23; Mark 8:27–33; Luke 8:18–22).

'Who do people say that I am?' asks Jesus.

The disciples reply, 'John the Baptist, or one of the prophets.' In other words, they are saying, 'Those who see what you do, and hear what you say, believe you are like the prophets of old, someone who speaks the word of God and who has extraordinary access to the power of God. They think you are an amazing person, like other amazing people they have heard about.'

'But who do you say I am?' Jesus persists.

It is then that Peter speaks up. He makes a declaration about Jesus, the significance of which he could not have realized at the time. It is one of those moments many of us experience occasionally, when a voice we know to be our true voice speaks from deep within, but it takes us by surprise because it is not something we expected to say. As we give voice to this deep expression of belief we are moved powerfully forward in our understanding of ourselves and, in this case, of God. 'You are the Messiah,' says Peter (Mark 8:29), and in Matthew, Peter adds, 'the Son of the living God' (Matthew 16:16).

Peter makes the crucial faith connection: Jesus is not just a good man, a powerful speaker, a brilliant teacher, a charismatic healer – he is the one through whom God will act to bring his reign to earth, the one to whom all Scripture has pointed, who will embody all it means to be the chosen of God.

It is therefore no coincidence that Jesus begins to teach Peter and the other disciples about the character of his messiahship as soon as Peter makes this declaration of faith. Jesus' messiahship is not to be as they expected: 'the Son of Man must undergo great suffering, and be rejected by the elders, the chief priests, and the scribes, and be killed' (Mark 8:31).

Peter then rebukes Jesus. Perhaps it seems to Peter that Jesus is being unnecessarily pessimistic. This apparently negative assessment of what will happen to the Messiah is at odds with Peter's own understanding. He has to learn that the way of Jesus is to be a different way, one of suffering, which leads to the cross.

This eventually becomes the great message of the early church. The cross that was the stumbling block for the Jews (because of their understanding of Scripture and their belief about the Messiah) and folly for the Greeks (how could a crucified teacher have anything worth saying?) was in fact the power and the wisdom of God, communicated through weakness (see 1 Corinthians 1:18–25). Hence, another verse from the psalms became very significant for the early church in interpreting what had happened to Christ:

> The stone that the builders rejected
> has become the chief cornerstone. (Psalm 118:22)

Jesus quotes this verse at the end of the parable of the Wicked Tenants (Mark 12:1–12). Having killed the slaves who come to collect the master's share of the produce from the vineyard, the tenants then kill the son, thinking they will inherit the vineyard. But the master destroys the wicked tenants and gives the vineyard to others.

When Peter is brought before the high priest, Caiaphas, and his council to account for the healing of a crippled beggar, Peter also quotes this psalm:

> Let it be known to all of you, and to all the people of Israel, that this man is standing before you in good health by the name of Jesus Christ of Nazareth, whom you crucified, whom God raised from the dead. This Jesus is 'the stone that was rejected by you, the builders; it has become the cornerstone.'
>
> There is salvation in no one else . . . (Acts 4:10–12a)

Here is a clear example of the first Christians using the Old Testament to make sense of what happened to Jesus. In doing this they are also addressing issues surrounding the right interpretation of Scripture, the nature of Jesus' messiahship, and therefore the nature of God's kingdom. After the cross and the resurrection, as they tell the story to others, their mission (especially to their Jewish brothers and sisters) is to tell the story with such reference to the Old Testament that the continuity between the revelation of God in the Law and the Prophets and the history of Israel, and the particular revelation of God in Christ, is established and clarified.

The concern both to win the argument over the issue of Christ's suffering and death and also to demonstrate the continuity of God's revelation informs the thinking of the early church. It shapes the way the Gospels were written. Sometimes the connection is made explicit in phrases that state this happened 'in accordance with the scriptures'.

Hence, when Paul reminds the church in Corinth of the basic facts about the Christian faith he uses these words: 'For I handed on to you as of first importance what I in turn had received: that Christ died for our sins in accordance with the scriptures, and that he was buried, and that he was raised on the third day in accordance with the scriptures . . .' (1 Corinthians 15:3–4).

John tells us that Jesus' thirsting on the cross is not just the dehydration and pain that is inexorably winding his life to its painful end: it is also in accordance with Scripture, a window into the very purposes of God. In other words, John is concerned not only with telling us about the pain Jesus is enduring (though as we have already discussed in the first chapter, this sharing in the human condition is a vital starting point for our understanding of who Jesus is); he also wants to reinforce his central claim that Jesus is God's Word made flesh.

Walking to Emmaus

Another fascinating example of Old Testament interpretation in the light of Jesus' death and resurrection takes place on the evening of the first Easter day as the risen, but unrecognized, Jesus accompanies two of his disciples on their journey to Emmaus (Luke 24:13–35).

Luke does not tell us why the two disciples have left Jerusalem, though it is fair to assume they are trying to escape the aftermath of the crucifixion for Jesus' followers. John's Gospel tells us the Eleven locked themselves away, fearful that what happened to Jesus might happen to them also. Jesus' death caused much anxiety and confusion, so perhaps these two decided to leave while the going was good.

As they walk, Jesus comes alongside them. At first they do not know him. We are not told why, though Luke care-

fully uses the phrase 'their eyes were kept from recognizing him' (Luke 24:16). Luke implies that this lack of recog-
nition is more then merely grief and disappointment dulling
their senses; it is God's intention that they do not yet see or
understand. It is also hardly likely that they expected to see
Jesus. After all, he had died two days before – he was the
last person they expected to meet! But also their expectations of a Messiah had been confounded.

Jesus asks them what they are discussing, and they
explain how they had hoped that Jesus, who had been executed that weekend, would be the one to redeem Israel
(Luke 24:19–21). In other words, they had placed a lot of
trust in this man called Jesus, and their hopes had been
dashed. They thought Jesus was the Messiah, but when it
came to the crunch he had not acted the way they had
wanted, or expected, him to. He had gone and got himself
killed, and from all accounts he had done little to resist. It
was as if he had just given in.

They then recount a strange story. That very morning
some of the women in their group had gone to Jesus' tomb
and had found it empty. Moreover, they had seen what they
described as a vision of angels saying he was alive. Not trusting the testimony of women, some of the men had also
gone to the tomb, and they too had found it empty, though
they saw nothing of Jesus.

Up until this point Jesus has patiently listened to all
that Cleopas and his companion have had to say. Now he
speaks, and his reply focuses immediately on the issue preventing them from receiving all they have experienced and
heard as good news, namely the nature of Christ's messiahship: 'Was it not necessary that the Messiah should
suffer these things and *then* enter into his glory?' asks Jesus
(Luke 24:26; my emphasis). Then, beginning with Moses

and all the prophets, Jesus begins to reinterpret the Scriptures for them, showing the passages about himself, uncovering a new way of looking at Scripture that points to a different messiah, a different kingdom.

If only we were able to eavesdrop on that conversation on that Sunday afternoon! For anyone who has sometimes found Bible study boring, imagining Jesus breaking open the Scriptures must surely be the antidote. In his study of Luke 24, *The Lord Is Risen*, this is precisely what Steven Croft does: he imagines what passages Jesus would have referred to, and opens up their relevance for this conversation and for our own understanding of Jesus' mission.[1] In particular, he focuses on the four Servant Songs (as they have come to be known) in the second half of the book of Isaiah. These chapters (40–55), normally ascribed to an unknown prophet, were written at a time of great suffering for the people of Israel, towards the end of the period when they were in exile in Babylon. From this darkness a different sort of hope emerges. No longer is it just concerned with the restoration of the nation, the re-establishment of the temple, a return home; it is also a vision for justice in all the earth.

'The person who will bring about this hope is no longer described as an all-conquering king who will enforce his rule on others, but a gentle servant, called and chosen by God, and now presented to the world.'[2]

> Here is my servant, whom I uphold,
> my chosen, in whom my soul delights;
> I have put my spirit upon him;
> he will bring forth justice to the nations.
> He will not cry or lift up his voice,
> or make it heard in the street;
> a bruised reed he will not break,

and a dimly burning wick he will not quench;
he will faithfully bring forth justice.
He will not grow faint or be crushed
until he has established justice in the earth;
and the coastlands wait for his teaching. (Isaiah 42:1–4)

There is not space here to go through all the Servant Songs, but each paints a picture of a servant who 'accomplishes more through suffering than can be gained through conquest'.[3]

Christians cannot read the fourth song (Isaiah 52:13 – 53:12) in particular without bringing to mind both the event and the meaning of Jesus' crucifixion. In its original context the poem seeks to find some meaning for the immense suffering Israel is experiencing. But the passage is an enigma within Judaism; the intensely individualistic nature of the prophecy is most unusual. In fact, it is hard not to draw the conclusion that it is only intelligible in the light of the Christian revelation of a truly righteous servant in whom the mysteries of vicarious suffering (the great theme of the end of this passage) become a witnessed fact. Although the New Testament quotes the passage in only a few places (we will look at one of them in a moment), it is clearly a foundational passage for the theme we are dealing with here and therefore worth quoting at some length.

As you read it, could I also ask you to adopt a different manner for your reading? Usually, when we read a book like this we scan down the page, not lingering much on each word, and often just getting the general gist of what the author says. But this piece of Scripture is a poem, and we best read poems repeatedly and thoughtfully. Pause, and if it isn't too embarrassing, read the words aloud. Let them sink into you, taste each one carefully, and allow their meaning to speak to you personally before you read on.

Indeed, it would be good if each extended piece of Scripture in this book were read in this way. If we simply race on through it, we lose a lot of the meaning. And this is doubly so if it is a familiar passage.

> He had no form or majesty that we should look at him,
> nothing in his appearance that we should desire him.
> He was despised and rejected by others;
> a man of suffering and acquainted with infirmity;
> and as one from whom others hide their faces
> he was despised, and we held him of no account.
> Surely he has borne our infirmities
> and carried our diseases;
> yet we accounted him stricken,
> struck down by God, and afflicted.
> But he was wounded for our transgressions,
> crushed for our iniquities;
> upon him was the punishment that made us whole,
> and by his bruises we are healed.
> All we like sheep have gone astray;
> we have all turned to our own way,
> and the Lord has laid on him
> the iniquity of us all.
> He was oppressed, and he was afflicted,
> yet he did not open his mouth;
> like a lamb that is led to the slaughter,
> and like a sheep that before its shearers is silent,
> so he did not open his mouth.
> By a perversion of justice he was taken away.
> Who could have imagined his future?
> For he was cut off from the land of the living,
> stricken for the transgression of my people.
> They made his grave with the wicked
> and his tomb with the rich,
> although he had done no violence,
> and there was no deceit in his mouth.

Yet it was the will of the LORD to crush him with pain.
When you make his life an offering for sin,
he shall see his offspring, and shall prolong his days;
through him the will of the LORD shall prosper.
Out of his anguish he shall see light;
he shall find satisfaction through his knowledge.
The righteous one, my servant, shall make many righteous,
and he shall bear their iniquities.
Therefore I will allot him a portion with the great,
and he shall divide the spoil with the strong;
because he poured out himself to death,
and was numbered with the transgressors;
yet he bore the sin of many,
and made intercession for the transgressors. (Isaiah 53:2b–12)

This beautiful poem tells of a redemption achieved at great cost. Again and again the writer tells us that the suffering of God's servant is for 'our sake'. The servant who is silent before his accusers brings forgiveness of sins for all nations, and out of the suffering there is also hope. Out of anguish the servant will see light. The righteous one will make many righteous.

The first Christians found in this passage a way of interpreting Jesus' death that showed he was the chosen of God, the servant, the Messiah.

We can only speculate about which passages Jesus shared on the road to Emmaus. But undoubtedly this passage from Isaiah quickly became of profound importance for the church in showing that the death of Jesus, and therefore the idea of a suffering messiah, a servant king, was in accordance with Scripture.

It is also interesting to note that Jesus does not give the two disciples any new information. Rather, he gives them a new interpretation. They already have all the information they need – they know about Jesus, they know about the crucifixion, they have even heard stories of the resurrection. But because of their beliefs about the way God would act to bring in his kingdom, none of this appeared to them as good news. The rather easy way in which Jesus had so allowed himself to be handed over to humiliation and death baffled them, and only made them feel they had got Jesus all wrong, that they had been mistaken to put such trust in him. Now, to offer them a new understanding and a radically different picture of God, Jesus takes them back into the Scriptures that have shaped their beliefs.

So riveting is his exposition of the Scriptures that, as night begins to fall, they invite him to stay with them. As he breaks bread with them at table and says the blessing (words and actions familiar from many earlier occasions), their eyes suddenly open. They see that the stranger who has walked with them all afternoon, and led them into new insights about their faith, is himself the risen Lord, the servant of God they have been speaking about. Everything clicks into place, and they say to each other, 'Were not our hearts burning within us while he was talking to us on the road, while he was opening the scriptures to us?' (Luke 24:32). That very instant they rush back to Jerusalem, eager to share with the other disciples the good news they have received.

When they get there, and are beginning to tell their story, Jesus again comes and stands in the disciples' midst. He shows them his hands and feet, the marks of his passion, and in so doing shows them the continuity between his suffering on the cross and the new resurrection life he brings. He has lived out what it means to be the servant of God, the thirsty one who is fully human and yet also God.

Unsurprisingly, the disciples are at first frightened and confused. Then Jesus begins to teach them, and he opens their minds to understand the Scriptures. 'Thus it is written', he says, 'that the Messiah is to suffer and to rise from the dead on the third day, and that repentance and forgiveness of sins is to be proclaimed in his name to all nations, beginning from Jerusalem. You are witnesses of these things' (Acts 24:46–48).

Philip and the Ethiopian eunuch

In another famous passage in the Acts of the Apostles the deacon Philip is inspired by the Holy Spirit to go to the wilderness road (another encounter with God on a journey) between Jerusalem and Gaza (Acts 8:26–40). There he meets an Ethiopian eunuch, a wealthy and important court official of the Candace, queen of the Ethiopians. The eunuch is reading from the prophet Isaiah. 'Do you understand what you are reading?' Philip asks. 'How can I, unless someone guides me?' the man replies.

The passage he is reading is chapter 53, the fourth Servant Song. 'About whom does the prophet say this?' the eunuch asks Philip, 'about himself or about someone else?' (Acts 8:34). Starting from this very piece of Scripture Philip then tells him all about Jesus, the one to whom this passage points, the one who alone makes sense of Scripture, the one who gives us a new interpretation of God. I expect he used words similar to those in 1 Peter, where the same passage from Isaiah is quoted: 'He himself bore our sins in his body on the cross, so that, free from sins, we might live for righteousness; by his wounds you have been healed' (1 Peter 2:24).

On the road to Emmaus the disciples required a new interpretation. This time, on the road to Gaza, it is information that is missing. The eunuch, deeply moved by the words of Isaiah, is obviously interested in the Jewish faith (we are told he has just returned from worship in Jerusalem), but he knows little or nothing about Jesus. So Philip shares with him the good news of what God has done in Jesus and no doubt tells him the story of the cross and the resurrection. The man is so stirred by what he hears that he asks for baptism, and, there and then by the side of the road, he receives the gospel's living water.

In both stories we can observe three features. First, both Jesus on the Emmaus road, and Philip on the wilderness road begin by listening. Jesus' first words to the two disciples are 'What are you discussing with each other while you walk along?' (Luke 24:17). These words display an amazing openness, and Jesus allows them to set the agenda. Philip asks, 'Do you understand what you are reading?' (Acts 8:30). He needs to know what this person makes of the scripture he is reading.

Second, both passages begin at the level of experience people have reached. The two disciples on the Emmaus road may well have been abandoning the rest of the group, looking to save their own skins. Jesus happily walks alongside them – while they are going in the wrong direction. Philip is prepared to leave behind the successes and rave reviews he is receiving in Samaria, where his ministry brings many to faith, and go to a lonely, desert road and with no idea whom he will meet there or what he is supposed to do. The man he meets is significant because, as a eunuch, he would not be allowed to convert to Judaism. But this does not prevent him becoming a follower of Christ.[4]

Third, there is a connection between the revelation of God in the Old Testament and the revelation of God in the New (though by 'New Testament' we are not yet referring to a book, but to the 'new' thing God has done in Jesus Christ). On the Emmaus road a new interpretation of the

Old Testament prepares the way for the acceptance of the New. On the wilderness road the new information about what God has done in Jesus, and the news of a reconciliation and relationship with God that breaks down the old barriers between Jew and Gentile, slave and free makes salvation available even to an Ethiopian eunuch, a Gentile outcast.

The Lamb of God

At the beginning of John's Gospel, John the Baptist proclaims Jesus to be 'the Lamb of God who takes away the sin of the world' (John 1:29). As we will see in the next chapter, Jesus himself had pondered long and hard on how he was to live out his vocation as the servant of God, and it seems likely that the Servant Songs in Isaiah were crucial in helping him work this out. Now they also open up to the first Christians a way of seeing and understanding Jesus' death and resurrection. Jesus is the lamb led to the slaughter, silent before its shearers, the one cut off from the land of the living, stricken for the transgression of God's people, by whose wounds we are healed.

The concept of the Lamb of God runs right through the Old Testament. When Abraham lifts the knife to sacrifice his own son, Isaac, God bids him spare the boy, and promises that he himself will provide a lamb for the sacrifice (Genesis 22:1–14). Jesus is that lamb. And he also represents the Passover lamb whose death and sprinkled blood spares the people of God from death (Exodus 12:1–28). If you remember the story of the exodus, God tells the people of Israel to take some of the blood from the lamb they have slaughtered and to paint it on the doorposts and lintel of the houses where they are eating the Passover. The blood on the houses will be a sign, and the Lord will 'pass over' the houses where the Israelites live; that is, he will avert his destruction from them. That night is the night of their liberation. The Passover meal, to this day, is celebrated as a day of solemn remembrance of this liberation. To be the lamb of God is therefore to be the one who brings liberation.

Hence, the whole story of the gospel is understood, proclaimed and recorded with constant reference to the unfolding drama of God's involvement with his people in the Old Testament. The death of Jesus, and the meal of the Eucharist that represents and celebrates that death, are the new Passover and the new exodus. Jesus himself is the Lamb of God.

John, in his Gospel, even carefully times the crucifixion so that the killing of Jesus on the cross happens at the same time that the Passover lambs are being slaughtered in the temple. This is why the chronology in John is different from the other Gospels: he emphasizes this link with the Old Testament; Jesus is the Passover lamb, he says. Jesus is the one set apart to be made holy (the literal meaning of the word 'sacrifice'). His death fulfils the Scriptures, for many of its details have a significance echoed in the Old Testament.

Therefore knowing that all was now finished, and in order to fulfil the Scripture, Jesus says, 'I am thirsty'. A jar full of sour wine is nearby, so the soldiers put a sponge full of the wine on a branch of hyssop and hold it to his mouth. Receiving the wine, Jesus says, 'It is finished', bows his head and dies.

Giving a dying man crying out in thirst vinegar to drink seems a cruel mockery. The reference to Psalm 69 would lead us to interpret it this way, and Luke in particular seems to understand it this way. 'The soldiers also mocked him, coming up and offering him sour wine,' he recounts (Luke

23:36). John's purpose, as we have seen, is much more concerned with the fulfilment of Scripture than with the intention of the act. But in all probability the soldiers giving Jesus sour wine to drink is best understood as an act of mercy. That is how Matthew and Mark seem to understand it. As Jesus cries out in desperation, even though they misunderstand him (they think he is calling on Elijah, when he is actually crying out that God has abandoned him), the soldiers can hear the pain in his voice and offer what comfort they can (Matthew 27:48; Mark 15:36). In which case, the reference to Psalm 22 is closest to the reality of what is happening. As we have already noted, this is the psalm that begins with these words of abandonment 'My God, my God, why have you forsaken me?' (Psalm 22:1). Jesus' heart is melting within him, his mouth drying up like a potsherd – a broken piece of pottery left out in the sun – his tongue sticks to his jaws: he is lying in the dust of death.

The sour wine offered was a kind of opiate called *posca* – a soldiers' brew made of wine, vinegar, water and beaten egg. Though there is some textual confusion here, which makes the precise meaning of the words unclear, the branch of hyssop was probably attached to a spear or javelin and lifted up to Jesus to dull the pain and quench his thirst. In the Greek the words 'hyssop' and 'spear' are similar. But a branch of hyssop, used in ritual cleansing has its own significance, and being a plant with a weak stem would have had to be attached to something stronger to be lifted up to Jesus.

That it happened according to Scripture tells us something profound about the purposes of God from the beginning in revealing his love and his intentions for the world. He chose a people whom he could shape in his way and nurture by his love; and then through the trials and delights of their history eventually act through them in the person of his Son, Jesus Christ. The story of the cross is the story of God's purpose to reveal his nature in the only way we could ever fully understand and receive it: through a man like us. Thus the promise of a messiah entrusted to the people of Israel, and largely misunderstood by them, was in the end the promise of God's own passionate involvement with the world he made.

That it happened according to Scripture also tells us something about the way the writers of the New Testament understood the Old Testament and constructed the narratives of the gospel. Because Christ was the fulfilment of the Old Testament, these passages, which so resonated with what they had experienced in Christ, would help the New Testament writers shape the telling of the story.

Implications for Today

I want to explore two implications that arise from our considering the words 'I thirst' as a fulfilment of Scripture, both to do with listening. First, listening to the word of God in the Bible. This should be fundamental to all Christian life, but it is often neglected. Lent is a time to renew our commitment to reading the Bible, and to think how the Scriptures can shape our lives. But, as we have observed already in this chapter, listening is fundamental to all healthy relationships, and God speaks to us in many ways.

We all know how good it is when someone listens to us. We also know how rude and unfriendly it feels when people don't. Therefore, we will also think about how we can listen to God speaking in the world around us, particularly through other people, and how God challenges and expands our understanding of faith through these encounters.

Listening to God's Word

The first Christians and the writers of the New Testament listened hard to the witness of God recorded in the Old Testament. They lived and breathed the word of God as recorded in the Scriptures.

We too should love the Bible more, and listen more attentively to the voice of God as it is spoken to us through the Scriptures. The Bible is far more than a book: it tells the story of the unfolding drama of God's involvement with the world; it shows us his love and purposes; it is a rich and complex library of poems, prophecies, letters, biographical narratives, histories and much besides. We should resolve to read and understand the Bible more.

By looking at these words of Jesus from the cross as a fulfilment of Scripture we are led to see that Christ himself is the centre of Scripture. All of Scripture points to Christ and it is through the revelation of God in Christ that we interpret Scripture. 'That is easy to see in respect of the New Testament,' says Steven Croft. 'Each of the books and letters is in some sense about Jesus and responding to his life, death and resurrection.' But the claim is also being made that Christ 'is the centre of the book we know as the Old Testament: the law, the prophets, and the psalms ... For this reason, the Christian Church has always been careful to see the Old Testament through the lens of the New Testament and of the gospel.'[5] If this is the case, then reading and understanding the Bible is not always going to be straightforward. On the one hand, this is a comfort – not many of us ever imagined it was going to be easy! But on the other, it is problematic: how are we to interpret the Scriptures, especially when it comes to controversial issues where Christians disagree with one another?

One of the ways forward is through study. Understanding how the Bible came to be written, the type and nature of its different books, and the different purposes and circumstances of individual authors will help us in the task of interpretation. Even a single verse like the one we examine in this book reveals the important insight that, in writing his Gospel, John is doing more than simply describing events. He interprets what he describes, and his primary tool is the Old Testament Scriptures. He sees Christ at the centre. He sees the Old Testament pointing towards Christ. He considers his experience of Christ, and apostolic witness of the first Christians, to be the yardstick for interpreting those Scriptures. Nevertheless, the Old Testament, just like the New, is a collection of books, a library. And as with any library, how you interpret the contents will depend upon which section you are in. So your approach in interpreting a poem will be very different from the way you handle a piece of history, or a recipe and so on.

In particular, the challenge here is to see Jesus in the Old Testament. Augustine famously said that 'the New is in the Old concealed, the Old is in the New revealed'. As you look at passages from the Old Testament, what do they tell you about Jesus?

The first of the traditional Lenten disciplines we looked at was fasting. I want now to speak about a second, namely, attending to the word of God. We are invited to the observance of a holy Lent by 'reading and meditating on God's holy word'.[6] In other words, it is not just about reading the Bible, still less with how much you read: it is about meditating on God's Word – listening hard to the voice of God speaking through the Scriptures – and then applying this in the individual circumstances of your life.

Make a commitment this week to read the passages set for this coming Sunday, and, having read them, spend time chewing them over, considering what they have to say to you. See if any word or phrase jumps out at you, and, if it does, make a note of it and go on pondering it through the week. Equally, don't worry if nothing strikes you as particularly interesting. Ask yourselves these two questions of the passage:

1 What does it tell me about God?
2 What does it tell me about how I should live my life as a Christian?

Or find other ways to make regular reading of and reflection on Scripture part of your ongoing spiritual life.[7] While Bible reading notes can be helpful, so too can the techniques for reflecting on God's Word suggested for the group exercises each week. There are other suggestions about reflective ways of reading the Bible at the end of this chapter. Inspect them and see if you find them helpful.

Listening to the world

A second implication concerns the way we listen to others. The first Christians and the New Testament writers listened hard to the objections and difficulties people had in understanding how the prophecies of the Hebrew Scriptures led to Jesus. We saw this illustrated well in the way Jesus responded to the disciples on the Emmaus road. First, he listens to what they have to say. He lets their questions and concerns set the agenda (Luke 24:17). Likewise with Philip: he goes to where the other person is and begins with the passage he is reading. In both cases the good news communicated is not just the message of the gospel, but the *manner* in which Jesus and Philip dealt with people.

We need to do the same today. We must meet people where they are, to listen before we speak. We need to *be* good news in the way we approach and deal with others, before we can *speak* good news. We need to meet people where they are because most people, however interested they are in the things of God, are still far from coming to church. If someone has never been to church, the first step into a Sunday service is often too daunting for that person to take unaccompanied. When we meet people where they are this is a vivid, practical expression of God's love. We listen to their concerns because the Christian faith is about the whole of life and we should not compartmentalize it into 'church' or 'Sunday': Christianity has something to say to every person and every situation. But the crucial point here is that we will never fully discover what this good news can be unless we first listen to the questions, concerns, passions and interests people have. Therefore, in our day to day dealing with friends and neighbours, work colleagues and family we need to live lives that demonstrate our readiness to listen and to serve, and then (because we are also listening to the voice of God in Scripture and to the way we can live out the Christian faith in our own lives) we will find we have something worth saying, something that can connect with the issues people face in their daily lives. In this sense the gospel can never be a disembodied package of truths to believe in. Just as it was incarnated in Jesus himself, so it is to be incarnate in us. Only by receiving, living and sharing it do we begin to understand it. Think of the gospel as a shining, multifaceted jewel. Some of it we can see, but much is still hidden. The new questions and new perspectives of others reveal to us new and beautiful facets of its truth.

And the questions people ask also change from generation to generation and from person to person. Nowadays people do not reject the claims of the Christian faith because they do not match up to their understanding of Hebrew prophecy. Other objections and stumbling blocks hinder them from embracing faith. A question you will often hear today is why a loving God allows so much suffering. As we explored in the last chapter, just because there is no easy answer to this question does not mean we have nothing to say: the one who fulfils Scripture is also the one revealed to us as the suffering servant, the one who shows us that God suffers too, the one who can make sense of suffering by bringing it to resurrection and eternal life.

Too often the church's proclamation of the gospel can be caricatured like this: Jesus is the answer, now what was the question? Like all caricatures it reveals an alarming truth. By listening carefully to Scripture we discover that Jesus himself and the first Christians were never so crass in their own proclaiming of the faith. What they said was subtly different from one situation to the next. The reason it was different was because they had listened. They were so engaged with the people they encountered and the situations they found themselves in that new truths about the gospel were revealed and fresh impetus to establish God's rule of justice was discovered. Loving and attentive listening overflowed into passionate action.

A Final Thought

This little phrase 'according to scripture' became so important in defining how the church understood the development of its faith that it even found its way into the creeds of the church. When we say the Nicene Creed in the Eucharist on Sundays we make this statement about the passion, death and resurrection of Jesus:

For our sake he was crucified under Pontius Pilate;
he suffered death and was buried.
On the third day he rose again
in accordance with the Scriptures.

We might also apply the phrase to ourselves. How can we
live according to Scripture?

For Discussion

Reflecting on God's Word

1 Read Isaiah 53 aloud.

2 Spend some time in silence.

3 Invite people to speak aloud into the silence a word
or phrase that strikes them from the passage.

4 In pairs or small groups share with each other the
words and phrases that have been spoken and how
they connect with the story of the passion.

5 What other parallels can you discern between this
passage and the passion story in the Gospels?

Deepening our understanding of Lent

1 What opportunities are there in your church to
• find out more about the Bible?
• read and meditate on the Bible in small groups?

2 What do you need to do about this?

3 How can your church be more attentive to the
community in which you are set? What do you
discern to be the questions, objections and
stumbling blocks that prevent people from hearing
the good news of the Christian faith?

4 How can you become a listening church?

For Reflection

The word of God should lead us first of all to contemplation and meditation. Instead of taking the words apart, we should bring them together in our innermost being; instead of wondering if we agree or disagree, we should wonder which words are spoken directly to and connect directly with our personal story. Instead of thinking about the words as potential subjects for an interesting dialogue or paper, we should be willing to let them penetrate into the hidden corners of our heart, even to those places where no other words have yet found entrance. Then and only then can the Word bear fruit as seed sown in rich soil. Only then can we really 'hear and understand' (Matthew 13:23).[8]

Ways of reflecting on the Bible on your own
Meditation on one verse

1 Choose a suitable verse (something from the psalms, such as the opening verse of Psalm 23 or 62 would be good. Or maybe a verse from Isaiah 53).

2 Prepare to pray. Take time to be still.

3 Repeat the verse slowly to yourself for several minutes until it begins to become part of you. Think of it in context. If it's a prayer, address it to the Lord. If the words are from God, imagine him speaking them to your heart and life.

4 Take the first word or phrase. Turn the word over in your mind. Think about what it means. Give God space to speak to you.

5 When you come to the end of that word or phrase (after minutes or days), go on to the next. As God begins to speak to you follow his lead – not your own method.

Imaginative contemplation

This way of listening is especially helpful with passages from the Gospels.

- Choose the passage before you pray – preferably the day before – and read it through several times.
- Take some time to be still and remember God's love for you.
- Set the scene for the passage in your imagination. Picture the place.
- Use your senses imaginatively. What can you see, hear, smell, taste and feel.
- Set the people in the scene. How do they feel about each other? Where are you and whose side are you on?
- 'Play' the scene in your imagination as slowly as you can. Listen carefully especially to any words spoken by Jesus or to Jesus. Listen carefully to your own feelings – especially towards Jesus.
- Meet Jesus on your own after the whole scene has been played through.
- Listen to what he is saying to you. Share your feelings with him.[9]

For Prayer

As the days lengthen and the earth spends longer in the light of day, grant that I may spend longer in the light of your presence, O Lord, and those seeds of your Word, which have been long-buried within me, grow, like every-thing around us, into love for you, and love for people; to become a visible declaration of your lordship in my life. Grant, Father, that this Lent there may be a springtime for my life in Christ.[10]

CHAPTER 3

The Call to Be Thirsty

Save me, O God,
for the waters have come up to my neck.
I sink in deep mire,
where there is no foothold;
I have come into deep waters,
and the flood sweeps over me.
I am weary with my crying;
my throat is parched.

PSALM 69:1–3A

The Gethsemane story in John's Gospel is summed up in one defiant statement. On the night before his crucifixion, as he is about to be arrested, Jesus says to his accusers as they seize him, to Judas who betrays him, and to his disciples who try to protect him, 'Am I not to drink the cup that the Father has given me?' (John 18:11b). These words encapsulate his vocation. He has come to earth to drink the cup the Father gives him, to live out and fulfil the whole of Israel's longing for God, and to be obedient to God's will. The other Gospels have more to say about the struggle that led to this declaration, and we will explore them from the perspective of this crystallization of his mission. He is the one who thirsts.

His final night begins with a meal.[1] In Matthew, Mark and Luke's Gospel it is a Passover meal, the occasion when

Jewish people recall and celebrate their liberation from captivity, their birth as a people. Jesus accords it new significance. As he breaks the bread he says to his disciples that it is his body. As he pours the wine he says it is his blood. They don't understand what he means, but within only a few hours it will become all too clear: Jesus' body will be broken like bread, his blood poured out like wine.[2] These mysterious and dramatic words and actions at the Last Supper give the disciples a way of interpreting Jesus' death. They also become a new Passover – a way of celebrating freedom from the captivity of sin and death.

After the meal Jesus goes with the disciples to a place called Gethsemane.[3] The accounts in Matthew, Mark and Luke's Gospels are slightly different, but in each he takes Peter, James and John with him to one side and asks them to watch with him. According to Mark, Jesus is overwhelmed with bewilderment and horror. He speaks to his disciples of a sorrow by which his very life is being drained away (Mark 14:34). He throws himself to the ground in anguished prayer. Only Mark records Jesus praying that 'if it were possible, the hour might pass from him' (Mark 14:35).

We can also detect in the way the Gospel writers tell the story the influence of the same Old Testament passages we discussed in the last chapter. Jesus' agony in Gethsemane is echoed in the opening verses from Psalm 69 at the head of this chapter, but Psalm 22 says:

> Be gracious to me, O LORD, for I am in distress;
> my eye wastes away from grief,
> my soul and body also.
> For my life is spent with sorrow,
> and my years with sighing;
> my strength fails because of my misery,

and my bones waste away.
I am the scorn of all my adversaries,
a horror to my neighbours,
an object of dread to my acquaintances;
those who see me in the street flee from me. (Psalm 31:9–11)

Luke's version is briefer than Mark's. Jesus approaches his time of testing more calmly. In Luke he kneels down and prays (Luke 22:41). He tries to prepare Peter, James and John for what is about to happen: 'Pray that you may not come into the time of trial,' Jesus says to them (Luke 22:40). But the pain and anguish are the same. Indeed, in Luke we hear that the sweat falls from Jesus like great drops of blood (Luke 22:44).

Then comes the prayer at the heart of Jesus' distress. The words are similar in all three Gospel accounts: 'Father, if you are willing, remove this cup from me; yet, not my will but yours be done' (Luke 22:42). In Mark's version it is more intensely personal: Jesus addresses God as *Abba* (Mark 14:36), using the intimate, almost childlike, Aramaic word for 'Father', similar to the English word 'Daddy'. Rather than asking if God is willing to take the cup away, he half challenges God with the words 'for you all things are possible; remove this cup from me' (Mark 14:36).

But whatever the differences in the three accounts we are left with an astonishingly moving picture of the struggle Jesus goes through to be reconciled to God's will on the night of his arrest.

Part of this struggle is an agony of fear. He sees the cup the Father puts before him. He shrinks from the physical pain and torture it holds. But there is the even more painful foreboding that perhaps this is not really God's will, that perhaps there is another way.

Embracing the scorpion

In 1939, just after the start of the Second World War, the English painter Stanley Spencer conceived and began a scheme of 40 paintings depicting Christ's fast in the wilderness. It was one part of the great unfinished projects of his life: to create a 'church house' filled with paintings that combined the themes of spirituality and domesticity that dominated his artistic life.

This is what Spencer himself said about the paintings:

> In doing these paintings of *Christ in the Wilderness* it was my wish that they should have been seen separately: one for, and on, each day of Lent. I thought that if a little shrine or frame could have been made, so that each of these same sized canvasses could be placed in it and removed from it each day, that like a calendar, the changing every day of these paintings of Christ's 40 days and 40 nights fast would help a person during Lent. In these works I have regarded Christ's dwelling in the Wilderness as a prelude forming part of the Ministry (or an introduction of considerable duration). Except for the last days when he was tempted, I don't know of any statements which refer directly to his life during this period except the reference to his fasting. But there is evidence of an appreciation of nature and nature's ways in all his sayings . . . That being so, I have tried to visualize the being he is, and the life he lived from day to day using the sayings as a clue and guide. [4]

Although the whole series was sketched in outline, only nine were completed. Unfortunately, they cannot be seen in Britain, though one or two have become well known. They hang in the Art Gallery of Western Australia in Perth, but I had the joy of seeing them in 1991 at a large retrospective exhibition of Spencer's work at the Barbican in London.

The paintings, with their bold stubble-bearded Christ, quite unlike the pale Galilean of so much Victorian religious painting, are arresting and disturbing. In recent years I have used slides of the paintings in many talks I have given on spirituality.[5]

The themes of the paintings – the dry and seemingly barren desert as a place of encounter and discovery, Christ's affinity with the creation, the vivid portrayal of Christ's humanity, his brooding upon his vocation – speak cogently and powerfully to the longing in the church today for a deep, holistic and human spirituality. Christ is the one who thirsts and craves; the desert is a fecund place flowing with life. Each is based upon a text from Scripture, though the texts are not always given.

In one of the paintings Jesus squats in the arid dust of the desert, cradling a scorpion in his hands, while another scuttles at his feet. He gazes upon it with a mixture of sorrow and tenderness. He is sad: it is the scorpion's nature to sting. He is also filled with wonder.

It is not an easy painting to read, but having looked at it many times I have found that its portrayal of Christ has had a huge influence upon my understanding of Jesus' vocation.

To understand the painting, one has to consider which text from Scripture Spencer had in mind. This is one of the paintings where the text is not given. There are, however, only two occasions in the New Testament where scorpions are mentioned, both in Luke's Gospel, and I think it is clear that Spencer had both in mind. The first is Luke 11:11 (NJB), where Jesus says, 'What Father among you, if his son asked for a fish, would hand him a snake? Or if he asked for an egg, hand him a scorpion?' Well, the astonishing implication of this picture is, God our Father, that's who! Because it is Jesus, the Son of God, who holds a scorpion in his hands. He tenderly cradles that which could destroy him. Indeed, the scorpion Jesus is given will turn out to be an egg, in so far as a new creation will arise from his receiving its poison. God does not just give us what is best for us; he gives us what is right.

This, then, is a picture of Gethsemane. It is a picture of Jesus' struggle to accept and embrace God's will. 'Father, if you are willing, remove this cup from me' (Luke 22:42).

Jesus longs that there might be another way. He does not want to face humiliation. He is fearful of death. In the agony of Gethsemane we shudder, for the Jesus we see here offers a reassuring picture of a God who experiences fear and pain just like us, but it is also disconcerting, almost too human. A frightened Jesus is hard to look at. We would prefer him more straightforwardly powerful. We like God when he is almighty and all knowing. We like Jesus when he is teaching and healing. Now, when there is anguish and pain, he is much harder to look at, much harder to follow. Perhaps his disciples falling asleep is as much about their denial of what is happening as their tiredness.

Jesus is very human in the Garden of Gethsemane. He wants to know if there is another way to fulfil God's will, a way that will not involve conflict and pain. He asks his friends to stay awake with him to support him through these hours of doubt and trial, but they all fall asleep. Quite alone, scared and tired, Jesus pleads with God, 'Father, is there another way? I'm not sure I can drink the cup you're giving me.' These are feelings we all understand. How many of us, on the threshold of difficult decisions, or facing situations of conflict, or contemplating pain, have not uttered similar prayers. But even though Jesus feels as we do, he does not act like us. The first half of his prayer is all too human – if it is possible, take this cup away. The second is the perfect mirror of the divine intention, an astounding living out of the third petition of the Lord's Prayer – not my will be done, but yours. Even in the jaws of betrayal, abandonment, arrest, persecution, mockery and death Jesus is obedient to the Father's will.

This bending to the Father's will is doubly emphasized in Matthew's account when Jesus, after finding his disciples asleep, unable to watch with him, prays again, but this time uses the exact words of the Lord's Prayer: 'My Father, if this cannot pass unless I drink it, your will be done' (Matthew 26:42).

Some commentators on these passages have observed how unlike the stories of the early Christian martyrs this account of Jesus' agony is. The martyrs are nearly always portrayed as going to their death with calm serenity. But surely they too would have struggled to understand, receive and accept such a vocation. This moving and heart-breaking story penetrates to the core of Jesus' calling. From it we look forward to the cross; we see the way Jesus rises up from his prayer and sets his face against those about to destroy him. Isaiah says:

> I did not hide my face
> from insult and spitting.
> The Lord GOD helps me;
> therefore I have not been disgraced;
> therefore I have set my face like flint,
> and I know that I shall not be put to shame;
> he who vindicates me is near. (Isaiah 50:6b–8a)

Jesus arrives at a point where he is able to embrace what lies ahead. He holds the scorpion. Not that he in any way enjoys or desires pain, but he knows God will vindicate him. He does not know the details of the resurrection. If he did, he would be less than human, his passion a temporary setback, rather than God's complete involvement in humanity. Neither does he know the finer details about the cross – though its shadow falls heavy upon him as he awaits arrest. What he does know is that obedience to the Father means being taken to places he would rather not go. The deepest fulfilment of the will of God demands that he let go of the temporal desires that would satisfy his own longings and calm his own fears. He must cleave to God and God alone.

The second time scorpions are mentioned is at Luke 10:19 (NJB), the return of the Seventy-Two. Jesus had sent his followers out in pairs to heal the sick and proclaim the kingdom. They come back rejoicing and Jesus says to them, 'Look, I have given you power to tread down serpents and scorpions and the whole strength of the enemy; nothing shall ever hurt you.' But in Spencer's picture of Jesus holding the scorpion the power he demonstrates is not the power to tread it underfoot without being harmed; it is the power to *love* the scorpion.

The picture is therefore not just a picture of Gethsemane; it is a picture of the cross. It is no begrudging acceptance of God's will but a complete and total self-surrender to God's will. We can therefore detect another layer of meaning in Jesus' words from the cross. When he cries out, 'I thirst,' he fulfils the prayer of Gethsemane. In Gethsemane Jesus prays for the cup to be taken away; now, upon the cross, he longs to take the cup the Father offers and drain it to the dregs.

In the picture Jesus' fingers are swollen. His hands are painted as if they are a plaited loaf of bread. Perhaps there is an indication here of the link between the broken hands of Jesus breaking the bread that will become for us the means whereby we share his broken, risen life. I think, however, there is a more simple explanation. Cradling the scorpion in his hands, Jesus' fingers are swollen because it has stung him. His posture, squatting in the heat of the desert, is close to the birthing position of African women. His pain is the birthpangs of a new age: his wounds heal us. His hands are also carefully painted in the precise position, one hand over the other, that most of us use when we receive Holy Communion. For Jesus, the kiss of the scorpion's sting is his communion. He thirsts to do the will of God.

Discovering vocation

How did Jesus arrive at this understanding of his vocation to be the one who thirsts to do God's will, to be the one through whom God acts?

First, I believe it was a vocation that grew and developed within him as he came to understand the purpose of his life and calling. Otherwise, he would not have been human in any way recognizable to our own humanity. His struggle at Gethsemane clearly illustrates the struggle of accepting where vocation leads. It is not an easy thing. Knowledge of vocation is not the same as mathematical or observational knowledge. Jesus did not know that he was God's Messiah in the same way that we know that two and two make four, or that the sky is blue. Knowledge of vocation arises out of faith and prayer. It therefore involves struggle and discipline.

Knowledge of vocation requires a conscious seeking after God: a letting go of desires for personal gain. It is always relational. It is never held with such certainty that one can let go of the God in whom one is seeking to find purpose and direction. For Jesus this would have meant his faithful participation in the Jewish community of faith and, in particular, a profound meditation on Hebrew Scripture, finding there a way that made sense of his own innate sense of calling. Eventually this leads him, as it does those who follow him, to the particular and astonishing claim that he is the Christ.

The writings of Tom Wright are most helpful here. He argues in several of his books that Jesus consciously placed himself within Israel's prophetic tradition. In the early part of his ministry Jesus clearly acts in the role of a great prophet. Like the great prophets before him, Jesus' theme is the unveiling of God's kingdom. By this he did not mean a place called heaven that we go to after death, but the rule of God on earth. Summed up in the second petition of the Lord's Prayer, 'Your kingdom come on earth as in heaven', is the central agenda of Jesus' ministry. However, the way in which Jesus understands God's kingdom to be breaking in leads him beyond the role of prophet to an understanding of his ministry as Messiah: that he himself is to be the one in whom God will act decisively to bring his rule to earth.

There were, however, other options available to Jesus. By briefly looking at them we can begin to appreciate how strikingly different is Jesus' own vocation and where it came from.

Jesus could have sought God's kingdom by withdrawing from the everyday life of the world. This is what many holy people did in Jesus' day. Cutting themselves off from an unclean world, they sought a life of purity. We have evidence of their life from the writings discovered at Qumran in the 1950s, known as the Dead Sea Scrolls.

Jesus could simply have compromised with the world – it was not easy living under Roman occupation. Why not just try to make the best of a difficult situation? This was the way of King Herod and many of the religious leaders.

Finally, Jesus could have taken up arms against Rome in a holy war. There were many whose frustration and zeal led them down this path. Indeed, the desire to crush one's enemy or oppressor is a response of powerlessness and fear we are well aware of in the world today. One of Jesus' disciples, Simon, is named by Luke as Simon 'who was called the Zealot' (Luke 6:15), thus indicating his possible association with some such political movement to overthrow the occupying forces of the Roman Empire.

But even though these different ways of establishing God's rule form the climate in which Jesus lived, he does not choose any of them. He rejects the ways of separation, compromise or arms, just as at the beginning of the gospel story he had rejected the temptations of the devil. Then he had been tempted to seek a way of popularity and power. Again he sets a new and striking course, one characterized by the word 'vocation', because it arises out of a profound sense of call. Always Jesus allows himself to be led, rather than to lead: always God is at the centre, the God he knows as Father. It is this heartfelt awareness of God as Father, and the deep-seated conviction and knowledge that God loves him, that gives Jesus courage, enabling him to continue when other voices suggest other ways.

In Gethsemane he asks for the support of his friends, but he doesn't rely on it. It is God to whom he looks; it is in the knowledge that he is fulfilling God's will that he finds strength and affirmation. But it is also a way that arises from his reflection on Scripture. As Jesus looks back into Israel's Scriptures he finds there another kingdom model, equally Jewish, but now to do with a messiah who is destined to suffer, who will embody within himself what it is to be the chosen of God and through whom reconciliation will come to all God's people. In other words, those very passages we looked at in the last chapter in relation to John's writing of his Gospel, and indeed the whole way the early church understood and interpreted its message, are the ones that in all likelihood Jesus himself pondered as a way of making sense of his own vocation. And because of the messianic nature of these texts he came to see himself as much more than a prophet. Indeed, Jesus speaks and acts 'as if God's plan for salvation and justice for Israel and the world was being unveiled through him'.[6] Wright puts it like this:

> In Jesus we see the biblical portrait of YHWH [God's name in the Old Testament] come to life: the loving God, rolling up his sleeves (Isaiah 52:10) to do in person the job that no one else could do; the creator God giving new life; the God who works *through* his created world, and supremely through his human creatures; the faithful God dwelling in the midst of his people; the stern and tender God relentlessly opposed to all that destroys or distorts the good creation, and especially human beings, but recklessly loving all those in need and distress. 'He shall feed his flock like a shepherd; he shall carry the lambs in his arms, and gently lead those that are with young' (Isaiah 40:11). It is the Old Testament portrait of YHWH; but it fits Jesus like a glove.[7]

Put plainly, Jesus 'believed he had to do and to be for Israel and the world, that which according to Scripture only YHWH himself could do and be'.[8] He had to thirst for the salvation of the world with the selfsame longing of God. This vocation was formed in him by his understanding of the Scriptures and traditions of Israel, of which he is a part, and for which he believes himself to be the turning point; and by the affirmation of the God whom he knows as Father.

Let me give just one further example of how this understanding of vocation may have worked itself out. It is the example Wright uses several times, and it concerns the temple in Jerusalem.

At the centre of the Jewish understanding of faith and order in this period of Israel's life was the temple. It was the place where God dwelt with his people – the place of sacrifice, the place where sins were forgiven, the place where Israel's union with God was renewed and expressed. On the day after his triumphant entry into Jerusalem, at the beginning of what we call Holy Week, Jesus goes to the temple and drives out those who are buying and selling, and overturns the tables of the traders and moneylenders (Mark 11:15–19). It is a shocking episode in the gospel story, not least because it is the only occasion where Jesus seems to act violently. But we are unsure how to interpret it. It is all too easy to see it in moralistic terms: Jesus' judgement on the corruption and sharp practice of the temple. However, their business was a legitimate and necessary part of temple life. Without the changing of money and buying and selling of pure animals, sacrifices could not be offered.

Therefore, Jesus is concerned with something much more than merely reforming the financial practices of the temple. By banishing the traders from the temple courts Jesus effectively takes away the whole purpose of the temple, if only for a couple of hours. 'Without the right money, individual worshippers could not buy pure sacrificial animals. Without animals, sacrifice could not be offered. Without sacrifice, the Temple had lost its whole *raison d'être*.'[9] It is as if Jesus is saying the temple is no longer necessary. Not because it is corrupt, but because of the new thing God is doing, that Jesus himself is now the place where, and the means by which, the living God is present with his people Israel.

Acting in this way also places Jesus in a discernible prophetic tradition. The prophets would often use a symbolic action to underline their message and intent. In fact, Jesus' whole ministry is in many ways best understood as a series of prophetic and symbolic actions he then comments upon and challenges people to understand. In other words, he is not first a teacher who sometimes acts, but someone (like a prophet) in whom God is acting to bring in his kingdom. Everything he says is in some way or other a comment on his actions. However, as these prophetic signs start to take on deliberate messianic overtones, his followers get more nervous and the path of his ministry moves with a certain inevitability, of which he himself was aware, towards conflict with the very leaders of Judaism, that is, those who ran the temple, the institution at the heart of Israel which his presumptuous actions appear to ridicule and usurp.

His entry into Jerusalem on a donkey, for instance, is not the sign of gentle humility that we usually understand it to be (ordinary pilgrims would arrive on foot). Rather, it is the deliberate and hugely provocative laying down of a messianic gauntlet. The prophet Zechariah predicted that Israel's king would come riding on a donkey (Zechariah 9:9). Jesus enacts this prophecy in order to make a clear claim about himself, the significance of which would not have been lost on the Jewish religious leaders. In the British situation it is like the prime minister placing a crown upon his head. It is the taking of a symbol of power and authority that belongs elsewhere and applying it to oneself. These actions at the beginning of the last week of Jesus' life are shocking and audacious. They are for Jesus the culmination of his ministry. They encapsulate his purpose. With deep sorrow (Jesus weeps over Jerusalem as the great city comes into sight[10]) he knows that they are leading to conflict, and he also knows that this is the way God's chosen must demonstrate God's love and purpose. Therefore, the shadow of the cross is already falling.

John, in his Gospel, places the story of the cleansing of the temple much earlier in the narrative, at a previous Passover visit to Jerusalem. In the exchange that follows, Jesus declares, 'Destroy this temple, and in three days I will raise it up' (John 2:19). The Jews are bewildered by his words: the temple has been under construction for 46 years – how can anyone claim to build it in three days? John comments, 'he was speaking of the temple of his body' (John 2:21).

Jesus' reflection on what it meant to be the suffering one in whom God reconciles his people led him to believe that all God wanted to achieve through the temple was to be achieved through him, that all the Scriptures pointed to him. His vocation was to *be* the one he read about in Scripture. It is a bewildering and astonishing claim to make, but I can see no other way of making sense of the Christian faith. Either Jesus was just a prophet (and all the other claims about him were later accretions to what is really only the story of a great and determined man), or else he was God in disguise as a man (not really troubled by the temptations and doubts that characterize our searching for the right way to live), or, as I am saying here, he is 'the thirsty one' (the one who is God come down to earth, God in human flesh, the one who through suffering becomes the means of reconciliation, who through thirsting provides the living water).

Like all vocations, this doesn't land in Jesus' lap fully formed. It is tested over many years and worked out through many trials. In Gethsemane a turning point is reached. It is possible to turn back, to seek compromise, to withdraw. It is also possible to lash out or fight back. Jesus chooses the path that is the culmination of his vocation, and it becomes a turning point for the world.

Implications for Today

Jesus' agonizing prayer in the Garden of Gethsemane reveals that the way of love that is his vocation will be hard and painful. Jesus chooses to let go of all the other options, to lay aside power and might, and instead show the mighty power of love. And because his love is real, so is his suffering.

We too need to hand ourselves over to God's will. Not just when we face agonizing choices or times of trial, but in all the affairs of our daily lives. We too need to pray that we might follow God's will, and not our own. We too need to discern the path of our vocation.

The implications we will explore in this chapter are all to do with self-examination. Lent is known as a penitential season, so there needs to be an emphasis on repentance as part of our Lenten discipline. But, as we will see, this is not just about recognizing and confessing sin, vital though this is; it is also about bringing the whole orientation of life (the true meaning of repentance) under Christ's rule. This is the way we discover our own vocation: the ways in which we are called to follow Christ and express our discipleship. This in turn will lead us to consider briefly the place of spiritual direction in our lives, and see how the fruits of self-examination and repentance lead us to experience the great gospel paradox, that in losing our life we gain it.

Self-examination

The observance of Lent requires of us the discipline of self-examination; that is, examining our lives in the light of Christ.

The first effects of this will probably be repentance. As we become more aware of the various ways we fall short of being the people God calls us to be, and as we become more conscious of the unsettling and destabilizing effects of sin in our lives we will be brought to a moment where there is genuine sorrow for our sinfulness and a desire to repent and start afresh.

Sin is not a popular concept in today's culture. We don't so much want to be forgiven as understood. Rather than face up to the clear wrong-headedness of many of the choices we make in life, we construct plausible excuses that will explain why we did such and such a thing, and why, with the right level of support and understanding, we will not do it again. Clearly, much about our wrongdoing and wrong choices is shaped by our environment and upbringing and we ignore these influences at our peril. We do indeed need to understand more about the forces and values that have shaped our lives and allow them to be examined in the light of Christ. Much of what has shaped us will be good and appropriate, but there will also be things that have poisoned our spirit at the heart. Many people, for instance, carry through life racist attitudes that were formed at an early age. These need to be submitted to the will of Christ. Is it his way to draw such cruel distinctions between people? Is he not rather saying to us that we should value all people regardless of creed, colour or class?

But there are also those occasions when, clearly, consciously, cold-bloodedly and wilfully, we chose to do that which we know is wrong. Sin is real. Whatever the reason, most of us, like the apostle Paul, will have this sort of experience: we don't understand our actions; the very things we don't want to do are the things we end up doing, and the things we want to do are the things we neglect (see Romans

7:15). And we don't need to be a Christian to think like this. All people have had the experience of going to bed at night, unable to sleep, turning the events of the day over in their head and thinking, 'Why did I say that?' or 'Why did I fail to do the other?' It is normal to think these things. What is becoming less normal is to do anything about it. Yet unacknowledged and unrepented sin does not simply go away – it poisons our system, excusing the persistent sins of negligence, intolerance, unkindness, and orientating our whole approach to life in a fundamentally self-centred way. Indeed, sin is best understood as that tendency in human beings to put themselves first. It is not that we should not have proper regard and love for self; only that we should not separate our love of God and love of neighbour from love of self. It is when we put ourselves above God and above neighbour that we begin to sin. We start imagining ourselves to be the centre of the universe and our own needs to be more important than anyone else's. We start to follow those siren voices which tell us that other people and other issues do not really matter, and that nothing can be done about them anyway. Even if we carry on believing in God, he is no more the source and centre of life, the one upon whom everything else is contingent, but just a compartment in our life, blessing and sanctioning our own selfishness. Thus if sin remains unacknowledged and unrepented of it leads to a complete closing in of the person, a cutting off from the rest of humanity, a death to community, a greater and greater self-centredness, a neglect of everyone else.

Acknowledging sin, seeking forgiveness, is the right way of responding. It is the way to health.

The Christian faith is a way of unfettered love. The Christian gospel has at its heart a message of reconciliation. Because God is our loving Father there is nothing that he will not forgive if we come to him with penitent hearts. Indeed, such is his love that even where we remain impenitent, he remains ready to forgive. Love can do no other.

It is therefore not God's readiness to forgive that is in question, but our readiness to acknowledge sin and its debilitating effects in our life and then do something about it.

The ministry of reconciliation

There are many different ways in which we can bring our need for forgiveness to God. We can confess our sins anywhere and at any time. But that way of confessing sins and receiving absolution (known as the sacrament of reconciliation, whereby individuals, keenly aware of their need of God's grace, confess their sins to a Christian minister and receive the absolute assurance of God's forgiveness) is the best way, I think. It used to be thought of as rather high church, and not really Anglican at all. In recent years, however, Christians of all traditions have learned to value the objectivity of this encounter, the personal assurance that comes from speaking to another person, not to mention the helpful advice that comes when sin, and therefore reconciliation, is taken seriously in this way.

Confession is also joyous. I remember making my own confession when I returned to faith aged about 20. It took a long while to get out all the stuff that was troubling me and all the things I knew were getting in the way of my life with God. But at the end, when the priest had assured me of God's forgiveness, I went away with the deep knowledge that I was loved, that God knew me through and through and still loved me.

If you believe that making a confession of sin is the right way forward in your own journey with God, then speak to your minister about it. Lent is often spoken of as a penitential season: a time when, more than anything else, we face up to our own sinfulness and seek forgiveness. As I observed earlier, Lent originated as a time of preparation for those who were being baptized at Easter and for those who, having broken fellowship through sin, were going to be restored to the church's community. Also, in due course it was recognized that all Christians could benefit from taking more seriously the call to repentance and the assurance of forgiveness proclaimed in the gospel. One of the ways we are invited to keep Lent holy is by self-examination and repentance.[11]

However, self-examination is not just about sin and forgiveness. By examining ourselves in the light of Christ we are led to consider the whole direction in which our lives are moving. Absolution, properly understood, is not just about wiping away sin; it is also concerned with unveiling what is good. Forgiveness is a work of restoration, revealing within us the image of Christ that so often gets tarnished and obscured.

Discovering vocation

Children at school nowadays are encouraged from quite an early age to think about what they will do with their lives: what career choices they might make, what exams they need to pass. The criteria by which these choices are made are often to do with money, status and power. How much I will earn is all too often the first question asked.

Christian people need to allow God to exercise his rule over all of life. We need to submit to him all our choices and consider how best we can serve his kingdom by the generous use of the gifts and opportunities given to us. In this sense every Christian has a vocation. It flows from our baptism. It is renewed and restored by the discipline of self-examination and the regular confession of sin. Vocation is not just something so-called special people, like clergy or teachers, have; each of us has a vocation to become the person God calls us to be, and to respond to the needs of the world in the way we use our talents, money and opportunities.

Vocation is about 'living in response to the continually developing call of God'.[12] God has a purpose for everyone: he values every particle of his creation; he delights in the multifaceted beauty of each person.

Jesus did not receive his vocation as a fully formed picture of what his life would be. It will be the same with us: it is something God will work within us as we begin to respond to and ponder the meaning of his call for us, and also as we respond to the circumstances of our lives. The tools for this discernment will be the same as for Jesus: prayer, a pondering of Scripture, a generous use of time and talents, and a testing within the security and affirmation of a Christian community the things that seem to be of God. In other words, it will be those same Lenten disciplines we are seeking to rediscover on our journey through this Lent. As the words 'I thirst' lead us to see Jesus as the thirsty one, to see that this was his vocation, so we will begin to see the bearings of our lives redirected. Thus the Holy Spirit acts within us like an inner homing device plotting the course home, enabling us to discover what it means in our life circumstances to be true followers of Jesus. This will involve both small things (e.g. how we behave to those around us, how we temper our language) and big things (e.g. what we do with our money, and with our life).

Many church communities have favourite hymns. In the church where I used to worship in Huddersfield the hymn by Sr Donna Marie McGargill OSM was the one everyone seemed to like singing more than any other. Its first two verses begin:

> What do you want of me Lord?
> Where do you want me to serve you?
> Where can I sing your praises?
> I am your song.
> I hear you call my name, Lord,
> And I am moved within me.
> Your spirit stirs my deepest self.
> Sing your songs in me.[13]

These words not only spoke to us as individuals, they echoed the journey we had made as a Christian community through some times of radical change. It is a song about vocation, for the chorus affirms over and over again, 'Jesus you are the Lord. Jesus you are the way.'

We all need to be open and vulnerable to the questions 'Lord, what do you want of me? Where do you want me to go? What do you want me to do? How can I best serve you?'

This is also a prayer of great abandonment: it is not about what I achieve through my effort or ability; it is about what I receive from God; it is about what God achieves in me: 'Sing your song in me, Lord. You are my way.'

None of us quite knows where this risky sort of prayer will lead, but without it the Christian faith remains just a set of beliefs – or worse, a leisure-time activity, the thing we do on Sundays. By daring to offer such a prayer of complete openness to God's will the Holy Spirit rushes in to shape and guide us. We will not necessarily feel any different, but when in years to come we look back, we will discern the different direction our life has taken; we will become aware of the different doors of opportunity that have opened to us.

Sometimes this will mean facing great pain, or persecution. Sometimes there will be momentous decisions – our own gardens of Gethsemane.

Spiritual direction

As we begin to work out what this might mean for us we will need the prayer and guidance of others. No one can be a Christian alone. Through our baptism we are brought into a community of faith. Within this community we each need the wise counsel and spiritual support of others. This ministry is traditionally called spiritual direction – quite literally it involves directing the way of our spiritual life (and because we have submitted the whole of our life to Christ, therefore we mean by this the direction of everything). Sometimes it will include the specific confession of our sins and the assurance of God's forgiveness.

The pastor of your church is the obvious person with experience and authority for this ministry, but all Christians can support one another in this. Often there will be lay people in the church with gifts for prayer, for listening and for spiritual guidance. These people's gifts need to be cherished and used for the building up of the whole body.

Lent is a good time to reset the compass of our discipleship and to seek help in allowing God to be Lord of all our life by speaking with some trusted Christian friend or minister about the direction and content of our life.

The fruits of self-examination and repentance

It has been rightly said of all traditions in the church that what really matters is not the form and expression our faith takes, but the evidence of our believing in the lives we lead. In other words, how is our life in Christ bearing fruit?

There is one further aspect of the Gethsemane story it would be good to look at here. In each of the four Gospel accounts as Jesus is arrested one of those with him draws a sword and cuts off the ear of the high priest's slave. It is a horrid act of unnecessary violence. In John's account the disciple who does this is named: it is Peter, poor, impetuous Peter, so quick to promise his allegiance to Christ, yet so prone to get it wrong, his headstrong self-will as yet unconverted by the way of suffering love![14] Jesus turns on him. 'Put your sword back into its sheath,' he says. 'Am I not to drink the cup that the Father has given me?' (John 18:11).

As we have already observed, this one sentence is John's summing up of the Gethsemane story. It projects us straight to Calvary, and to the thirsting, suffering Christ upon the cross, resolved to do the Father's will. 'What should I say', Jesus challenges his disciples, '"Father, save me from this hour?" No, it is for this reason that I have come to this hour' (John 12:27).

But there is another, more incidental purpose. As I have written elsewhere:

> In our lives there are so many occasions where our instincts tell us to seek revenge, to exact retribution. Violence simmers just below the surface of the fragile equilibrium of our civilization. Only when we have learned to love our enemies and to face the cost of turning the other cheek will we learn to be like God and let our passions be directed on the path of love.[15]

Jesus' teaching, that we should love our enemies and pray for those who persecute us (Matthew 5:44) was shocking for the people of his day, as it remains shocking to us today. In so many ways we quite like a vengeful God. It can justify the rage and vindictiveness of our own actions. It allows us to excuse violence and turn our back on oppression, to excuse our spending vast sums each year on ever more sophisticated weapons. It means we can keep at arm's length the radical love Jesus shows us in his passion.

'Am I not to drink the cup that the Father has given me?' asks Jesus. Am I not to be the thirsty one? The loving one? He is ready now to receive the worst we have to offer. In Gethsemane, ready to show the world a better way, he is ready to drink the cup the Father gives him. Perhaps in Peter's wild act of violence Jesus saw again the desperate need for the world to learn a better way.

I also see in these words of Jesus evidence of his arrival at a point of complete openness to God. So often we wonder why God does not seem to act in and through us. So often it is because we have not even approached this attitude of surrendered vulnerability to God's purposes and love. We still seek other ways. But here Jesus has become the one thirsty for God.

Final Thought

In Luke's account of the Gethsemane story one detail does not appear in either Matthew or Mark. Having prayed that the Father might, if possible, remove the cup, an angel comes from heaven to give Jesus strength (Luke 22:43–44). Some Bibles put these verses in brackets, the footnotes telling us that some ancient versions of Luke's Gospel authorities do not have them at all. However, they are very interesting. Robert Warren in his book on the Beatitudes, *Living Well*, cites them as an example of the dynamic at work in the second Beatitude: 'Blessed are those who mourn, for they will be comforted' (Matthew 5:4).[16] At the time of his greatest testing, where Jesus is crying out to God in lamentation, he receives the assurance of God's comfort – the angel comes to strengthen him.

The literal meaning of the word 'comfort' is 'to give strength'. In Gethsemane, Jesus receives comfort – but not as we usually understand the word today. It is not tea and sympathy that he receives, but the courage to face what lies ahead. It is then that we are told Jesus' sweat fell like great drops of blood. The comfort has not made the pain any less real, nor the cup he has to drink any more appetizing. But Jesus now has fresh resolve to do what he has to.

In John's Gospel the Holy Spirit is referred to as the 'Paraclete' (John 16:7, and in other places), a word sometimes translated as the 'comforter': the one who will bring strength in times of trial. We need to pray to receive the strength of the Holy Spirit as we face the testing and temptation that strew our way and as we cry out against the world's injustice.

For Discussion

Reflecting on God's Word

1 Read in Luke's Gospel the story of Jesus praying in Gethsemane, his betrayal and arrest (Luke 22:39–53).

2 Spend some time in silence.

3 Invite people to speak aloud into the silence a word or phrase that strikes them from the passage.

4 In pairs or small groups share with each other
the words and phrases that have been spoken and
how they connect with your own experiences of
• discerning God's will for your life;
• reaching difficult moments of decision;
• receiving strength and comfort (what form
  did it take?);
• feeling betrayed and let down.

5 How does this story help you to make sense of your
own experience?

6 How do these experiences help you to understand
your own vocation and ministry?

And you may wish to discuss this next question in pairs
or threes rather than as a whole group:

1 Can you discern 'a cup' that God is asking you to
drink? Does this image in any way help you to focus
your own sense of God's calling for you at the
moment?

Deepening our understanding of Lent

1 How does your church help people face up to the
reality and consequences of sin, and how does it
practise the ministry of reconciliation? How would
your church be different if this ministry were at the
heart of its life? And what difference (if any) would
this make to the way the wider community
perceived your church?

2 How can you support each other in discerning
vocation, seeking God's will and practising
self-examination?

For Reflection

A Prayer of Self-Examination

Help me, O Holy Spirit, to search and question myself,
and honestly to answer:
Am I single minded in seeking my God?
in serving him? even in praying to him?
Do I put God first in deed? in intention?
or even in desire? in hope?
What reserves do I always maintain against him?
what other loves cling to?
Is not self-regard my prevailing motive,
secret, silent, undetectable, insatiable?
Where do I serve self in daily conduct,
when I should be serving others?
when I should be serving God?
Do I obey self even in the most inward, spiritual things?
in the exercise of holy ministries
even in the holiest place?
Search me thyself, O God,
seek the grounds of my heart;
Look well if there be any way of wickedness in me,
any subservience to mine ease,
any hungering and playing for mine own honour.
Help, O help me slay my self-regard,
the foe that is in myself and of myself,
and to want to slay it.
O Saviour of the world,
who by thy Cross and precious Blood hast redeemed us,
save and help me,
I humbly beseech thee, O Lord.[17]

A Brief General Confession

Almighty God,
long-suffering and of great goodness:
We confess to thee, we confess with our whole heart,
our neglect and forgetfulness of thy commandments;
our wrong-doing, speaking and thinking;
the hurt we have done to others;
the good we have left undone.
O God, forgive thy people
that have sinned against thee:
lay every barrier low between thyself and us
and raise us to newness of life;
through Jesus Christ our Lord. Amen.[18]

Once there was a very old man who used to meditate early every morning under a large tree on the bank of the Ganges River in India. One morning, having finished his meditation, the old man opened his eyes and saw a scorpion floating helplessly in the strong current of the river. As the scorpion was pulled close to the tree, it got caught in the long tree roots that branched out far into the river. The scorpion struggled frantically to free itself but got more and more entangled in the complex network of tree roots.

When the old man saw this, he immediately stretched himself onto the extended roots and reached out to rescue the drowning scorpion. But as soon as he touched it, the animal jerked and stung him wildly. Instinctively the man withdrew his hand, but then, having regained his balance, he once again stretched himself out along the roots to save the agonized scorpion. But every time the old man came within reach, the scorpion stung him so badly with its poisonous tail that his hands became swollen and bloody and his face distorted by pain.

At that moment, a passer-by saw the old man stretched out on the roots struggling with the scorpion and shouted: 'Hey, stupid old man. What's wrong with you? Only a fool risks his life for the sake of an ugly, useless creature. Don't you know that you may kill yourself to save that ungrateful animal?'

Slowly the old man turned his head, and looking calmly in the stranger's eyes, he said: 'Friend, because it is the nature of the scorpion to sting, why should I give up my own nature to save?'[19]

For Prayer

I was slow to love you, Lord
your age-old beauty is still as new to me:
I was so slow to love you!
You were within me,
yet I stayed outside
seeking you there;
in my ugliness I grabbed at
the beautiful things of your creation.
Already you were with me,
but I was still far from you.
The things of this world kept me away:
I did not know then
that if they had not existed through you
they would not have existed at all.

Then you called me
and your cry overcame my deafness;
you shone out
and your light overcame my blindness;
you surrounded me with your fragrance
and I breathed it in,
so that now I yearn for more of you;
I tasted you
and now I am hungry and thirsty for you;
you touched me,
and now I burn with longing for your peace.[20]

CHAPTER 4

The Tenacity of Love

O God, you are my God, I seek you,
my soul thirsts for you;
my flesh faints for you,
as in a dry weary land where there is no water.

PSALM 63:1

In this chapter we look closely at the passion of Jesus itself. John begins his account with these words: 'Having loved his own who were in the world, he loved them to the end' (John 13:1). He then tells the story of Jesus washing his disciples' feet. But this 'loving to the end' is not just a description of this acted parable of service. Nor is it just the precursor to Jesus giving them the new commandment: 'Just as I have loved you', says Jesus, 'you also must love one another' (John 13:34). The words 'he loved them to the end' describe the meaning of Christ's passion and death. Jesus is going to carry on loving right to the end. His death on the cross is the climax of his ministry of love.

Jesus has done all he can to show his disciples the way of love, but he must go this next mile himself. Handed over first to the Jewish authorities, and then to the Romans, he is silent before his accusers:

like a lamb that is led to the slaughter,
and like a sheep that before its shearers is silent,

so he did not open his mouth.
By a perversion of justice he was taken away. (Isaiah 53:7–8)

'My kingdom is not from this world', Jesus says to Pilate (John 18:36).

The accounts of Jesus' death in the Gospels are called passion narratives. This is because they are primarily concerned with Christ's suffering, the basic meaning of the word 'passion'. But this word has two other meanings that are relevant here. The word 'passion' is also used to describe love. We love passionately. It is a word that carries connotations of desire, ardour and excitement. The passion of Jesus is a demonstration of God's passionate love for the world, the depth of which is revealed in the suffering of Jesus.

The word 'passion' also shares the same root as the word 'passive', itself an obsolete term for suffering, but still retaining the idea of being acted upon, of not reacting, of refusing to resist. The passion of Jesus therefore reveals something astonishing about God. 'Love is patient; love is kind', says St Paul. 'It does not insist on its own way; it is not irritable or resentful . . . It bears all things, believes all things, hopes all things, endures all things. Love never ends' (1 Corinthians 13:4–8). This is the love we see in what we might dare to call the passivity of God revealed in the cross of Christ. Through his refusal to run away, fight back or have the last word Jesus shows us the capacity of love to endure all things. His silence before his accusers, his forgiveness of those who persecute him, his complete lack of hatred, most reveal the true nature of God's unconditional love. Do your worst, Jesus seems to say from the cross, and I will go on loving. And ultimately, in my dying and refusing to let your hate beat me, I will love you into submission, and you will learn to love in return.

This is the way Jesus chooses. The rapid unfolding of the events of his passion are both a triumph of love and a confrontation with the vilest powers of sin and evil.

The passion of Jesus

Late on the Thursday evening he is arrested. The Gospel accounts all differ slightly in the sequencing of the events that happen through the night. But on Friday he finds himself standing before the Roman governor, Pontius Pilate, accused of blasphemy and insurrection. Although most of Jesus' followers have abandoned him, some women disciples stay as close as they dare. However, basically, Jesus is alone.

Pilate is the one person who has power to save him, but Jesus offers no defence and the trial is a travesty. The crowd is stirred up against him. The religious leaders are bent on crushing him, and Pilate only wants the whole thing over. He probably does not want to have Jesus executed, but he is a weak man. Swayed by the crowd and probably eager to keep the peace with the Jewish religious authorities he has Jesus flogged. But this is not enough to satisfy the blood-lust now consuming the baying crowd. So, washing his hands of the whole affair, he sends Jesus out to be crucified.

The soldiers dress Jesus up as a kind of puppet king. As they lead him out, they bow and curtsy before him. He claimed to be a king, is the all-too-human logic of their mockery, so let's dress him up for the occasion: a purple robe around his shoulders, a twisted crown of thorns upon his head. We'll enthrone him on a cross, they joke.

Above his cross a sign is hung: 'Jesus of Nazareth, the King of the Jews' (John 19:19). And, so that everyone can get the joke, it is written in three languages – Hebrew, Latin and Greek. The chief priests complain – lest any humourless soul should imagine he really is a king – that the sign should read, 'This man *said*, I am King of the Jews' (John 19:21; my emphasis). But Pilate lets the inscription stand, a lone witness to love's victory in the appalling cruelty of the events about to unfold, a message in every language of the truth about Jesus.

We can read in each Gospel the chilling account of Jesus' death, but before we explore the meaning of that death, let us examine what actually happened.

What happened?

Crucifixion, in itself, was not a remarkable event in Jesus' day. It was the favoured method of execution for the Romans, an idea they had taken over from the Phoenicians. It was the standard penalty for serious crimes such as desertion, murder and high treason, and had become an instrument of terror as well as death. Many people perished on the cross, slaves, prisoners of war, criminals – sometimes thousands at a time. Only full Roman citizens were exempt.

The Romans liked it as a method of execution because of its precision. It produced the maximum amount of pain and a death struggle of adjustable duration. In fact, they had so mastered the technology of the cross that they could decide how much they wanted it to hurt and how long it would take someone to die. Over the course of a thousand years countless people died on countless crosses. We often hear talk today of precision weapons, but, sadly, there is nothing new about this. Human beings have always had a ghastly ability for devising ever more sophisticated and efficient ways of killing each other. Crucifixion was one. If you are squeamish, it might be better if you skip the next section, and continue from the section 'Light in the Darkness'.

The executions always took place in public – indeed, they were public events – and there were times when the

Romans' circus arenas became forests of crosses. After the defeat of the Spartacus uprising in 71 BC almost 6,500 crosses lined the Appian Way from Cappadonia to Rome. On each cross hung a rebellious slave or a gladiator. In fact, so common was crucifixion – and so feared a way of death – that the Gospel writers do not describe it much. Everyone in the Roman Empire knew all too well how it was done and what it involved.

Jesus did not carry the whole cross, as is usually shown in depictions of the story. After the soldiers had beaten and dressed him up as a king they gave him just the crosspiece, in Latin the *patibulum*, to carry. It was probably made of cypress wood and weighed about 34–57 kilograms (75–125 pounds), about as heavy as a bag of cement.

As Jesus carried this crosspiece we are told in Matthew, Mark and Luke's accounts that someone is taken from the crowd and enlisted to help him. The Gospel writers name him as Simon of Cyrene. Mark also adds the touching detail that Simon is the father of Alexander and Rufus (Mark 15:21). This is one of a number of small incidents in the New Testament that transport us instantly to the historicity of the accounts we are studying. Why would Mark add such a seemingly insignificant detail unless these two – Alexander and Rufus – were known to the community he was writing for? That the soldiers have to compel someone to help carry the cross, however, shows not only the heaviness of the weight Jesus is carrying, but also his physical weakness. Such help ensures that Jesus won't expire too quickly and deny the crowd the spectacle of death.

When they reach Golgotha, outside the city wall, Jesus is stripped (the Gospels add the nasty detail of the soldiers casting lots for his clothes) and then nailed to the cross. Popular depictions of the crucifixion usually show the nails driven through the palms of Jesus' hands. Actually, the nails were driven through the *wrists*: the palms could not withstand the weight of the body – they would tear through longways.

Bob Smalhout, a professor of anaesthiology at University Hospital, Utrecht, has researched the techniques and medical effects of crucifixion. Much of what follows is based closely upon his writings and research.[1]

The nails would probably be about 20 centimetres (8 inches) long. They were driven precisely into the space between the wrist bones. These were dislocated, but not shattered. If you have ever sprained your wrist you will know how painful it is, but, much worse than this, an important nerve, the median, crosses the wrist joint. The square-edged nails would almost always come into contact with the nerve, stretching it over the sharp sides of the nail like the strings over the bridge of a violin. This would cause such severe cramp in the thumb that it would bend violently, the thumbnail embedding itself into the flesh of the hand.

The next step was to hoist the victim and slot the crosspiece on to the vertical stem. Then the knees were bent until the sole of one foot could be pressed flat against the stem, and a 20 centimetre nail was driven through it, precisely in the middle between the second and third metatarsal bones. As soon as the nail emerged through the sole the other leg was bent into position so that the same nail could be hammered through the second foot and into the wood. The victim was then left to hang from three nails (the two through the wrists, and the one through the feet). Blood loss was slight, but the pain was unbearable. The death struggle had begun.

A body suspended by the wrists will, pulled by gravity, sag downwards. This produces enormous tension in the muscles of the arms, shoulders and chest wall. The ribs are drawn upwards so that the chest is fixed in position as if the victim has just drawn a large breath – but cannot breathe out. The condemned man begins to stifle.

The severely strained arm, shoulder and chest muscles develop agonizing cramp. The metabolic rate is raised, but the oxygen supply is reduced. One result of this is the production of large amounts of lactic acid in the bloodstream, leading to what is known as 'metabolic acidosis', often seen in athletes driven to exhaustion and severe cramp. This is aggravated by the difficulty in breathing and in ridding the body of carbon dioxide, leading to 'respiratory acidosis'. Unrelieved, the victim finally dies of suffocation. This can occur within half an hour.

A swift death, however, did not satisfy the Romans. This is why they nailed the feet too. It was a way of prolonging the agony. The condemned man could buy time by pushing himself up on the nails in his feet, stretching his legs and so raising the body to relieve the chest and arms. This allowed him to breathe better – for a while. But perching with the full weight of the body on a square nail driven through the middle bones of the feet brings intolerable pain. The victim soon lets his knees sag until once more he is hanging from the wrists, with the median nerves again strung over the nail shafts. The cycle is repeated to the limit of endurance.

So this is what happened to Jesus. He had to endure the torturing choice between suffocation and rending pain. The slow and deadly cycle followed its inexorable course for six full hours. No wonder classical Latin writers such as Cicero and Seneca described crucifixion as the most abominable method of execution of all.

Jesus' temperature soars. His muscles are in perpetual cramp. Sweat and blood run down his body and this excessive sweating brings with it severe thirst. His blood pressure falls. His heart pounds faster. By now the severely acidotic condition of his blood, combined with the excessive loss of salt through sweat, means that his body is barely hanging on to life. His heart begins to fail and his lungs fill with fluid. The beginnings of the death rattle croaks in each, failing, painful breath. Finally, the dying man calls out, 'I thirst'.

This is when the soldiers offer Jesus the *posca* – an act of mercy to the dying man – to dull his pain and slake his thirst. At any rate, we are told in John's Gospel that after it is drunk Jesus says, 'It is finished' (John 19:30). He then bows his head and dies.

Light in the darkness

The Gospels all speak of darkness covering the land as Jesus dies on the cross. In John's account in particular the whole passion story takes place in darkness. It emphasizes again the cosmic implications of what is happening. As Judas goes out to betray Jesus we are told that night has fallen (John 13:30). And now – in the middle of the day – we are still in the middle of darkness. This is the darkest hour in which it seems that death and sin and evil have spread their dark blanket over the word and extinguished love.

But this is also the hour of love's victory. On the cross Jesus confronts the powers of sin and death and darkness, for this is not just the death of a good and innocent man. This is not just about God sharing the suffering of the world. On the cross God redeems the world, promising eternal rest.

Thus the calmness of Jesus, despite the unimaginable agony of what he endures, is in stark contrast to the failings and weakness of so many others. The religious leaders only look to protect their own position. It seems to them expedient that one man should die rather than have the whole nation destroyed (see John 11:50). Pilate just wants an easy way out. Judas has probably already hanged himself. The disciples are either in hiding or have fled. Only a few of Jesus' followers, mainly the women in the group, make it to the foot of the cross. The crowd, who sang 'Hosanna' one day, now cries for blood. It seems we are witnessing the triumph of evil.

The triumph of love

In families, stories are often told about what different family members did in their childhood and how they behaved. In my family the story is often told about how I used to lose my temper, flying into an irrational rage at the drop of a hat. My mother also likes to recall how she dealt with my anger, not by shouting at me, not by meeting rage with yet more rage, but by loving me. She would confront my anger with a tenacious tranquillity. She would hold me, doggedly containing the fury within me. I can still remember how this felt. At first it would cause the anger inside me to boil even more furiously. But soon I would find it melting away. The cool embrace of love taming and conquering the frenzy within me. Her embrace absorbed my anger. Like a lightning conductor pulling the energy of the storm out of the sky and burying it safely in the earth, my anger was exhausted and dispersed. More than this, it was transformed (because this is what love can do). Eventually there is no rage left – not only am I loved, but I now love in return.[2]

This illustrates what happens on the cross. It is what I call 'the tenacity of love': Jesus keeps on loving those who keep on hating. He defeats sin and death by the resolute persistence of his love. To the soldiers who nail him to the cross he speaks words of understanding and forgiveness: 'Father, forgive them; for they do not know what they are doing' (Luke 23:34). To the thief who hangs alongside him he promises a share in Paradise (Luke 23:43). These beautiful words spoken out of the horror of the cross embody his life's teaching, that we should love our enemies, pray for those who persecute us, walk the second mile. It is the love that carries on loving, right to the end.

Yet there is terrible risk in this love. If Jesus had given in to the taunts and indignity and sheer bloody awfulness of the cross, then love would have failed. It would have become less than love, and less powerful than hate. But by allowing himself to be handed over to this passion, and by fulfilling the vocation of love, God triumphs. He triumphs in the all-too-human flesh that Jesus now redeems. He risks the possibility of failure, as today he risks the possibility that we may never recognize the nature of his triumph. But that is the way it is with love. All it can do is go on loving. It can never coerce, and it can never wantonly hurt or manipulate that which it loves.

The words 'I thirst' sum up this love because they witness to the frightful horror of what is happening – the indignity, the humiliation, the pain. But they also penetrate the deepest purposes of God. 'I thirst for *you*,' says Jesus from the cross. 'I do this for you: I am the faithful one who lays down his life for his friends. I do this for God: I drink the cup the father sets before me. I desire your salvation. Like a dry, weary land where there is no water, so I thirst for you and I thirst to do God's will. See how much I love you. See the depths of the Father's love. See my arms stretched out in love for you. Allow yourself to be embraced by my love. Allow yourself to be transformed.'

Sin and death are brought to submission by the persistence of Christ's love. All their forces are spent upon him, but he carries on loving. In the end the voices of the thief asking to be remembered in God's kingdom, the forgiven soldier at the foot of the cross recognizing by Christ's death that he is the Son of God, witness to love's triumph.

A great spiritual writer and theologian from the fourteenth century helps us penetrate the mysteries of this love. On 8 May 1373 Julian of Norwich received from God a series of revelations. Known to us as the *Revelations of Divine Love*, she wrote down twenty years later her account of what had happened to her and what it meant. It is one of the most beautiful and extraordinary spiritual works in the English language. Its constant theme is the love of God revealed in the passion and death of Jesus. Indeed, it seems to Julian that she stands at the foot of the cross, witnessing Christ's passion first hand and hearing him speak to her.

In the tenth revelation Julian sees the heart of Jesus riven in two. She sees 'a place, fair and delightful, large enough for all saved humankind to rest in peace and love.'[3] She hears Jesus speak to her, 'See how I have loved you . . . see the delight and happiness I have in your salvation.'[4]

Further on she speaks of Christ's thirst:

> This is his thirst: his love and longing for us that goes on enduring until we see the Day of Judgement . . . His thirst and loving longing is to have us all, integrated in him, to his great enjoyment. At least, so I see it. We are not as fully whole in him as we shall be then . . . Therefore the same desire and thirst that he had upon the cross – and this desire, longing and thirst was with him from the very first, I fancy – he has still, and shall continue to have until the last soul to be saved has arrived at its blessedness. For just as there is in God the quality of sympathy and pity, so too in him is there that of thirst and longing. And in virtue of this longing which is in Christ we in turn long for him too. No soul comes to heaven without it.[5]

Again and again Julian emphasizes that love is the meaning of the Christian faith, that the cross is where we see the tenacity of God's love for us. We can choose to ignore, or ridicule and deny, God's love, but we cannot stop him loving us. Whether we like it or not, we are his beloved children. His cross is not just the turning point of human history, the place where God reconciles all things to himself, the place of peace (see Colossians 1:20); it is the sign for all eternity of what God is like, 'the surest, truest and deepest window on the very heart and character of the living and loving God', as Tom Wright puts it.[6]

Love's judgement

If we are all created by God, does it follow that eternal life with God is automatic and it doesn't much matter whether we follow Jesus or not? Or to put it more bluntly, does everyone go to heaven? This is how the Church of England's Doctrine Commission answered this question: 'No one can be compulsorily installed in heaven. God whose being is love preserves our human freedom, for freedom is the condition of love. Although love goes on, and has gone, to the uttermost, plumbing the depths of hell, the possibility remains for each human being of a final rejection of God, and so of eternal life.'[7]

What about hell then? Someone asked me recently whether I believed in hell? I smiled, and said that I did, but I thought it was probably empty! What I meant was, that because being free is so fundamental to our humanity, we must be free to reject God. Therefore I believed in hell. However, because I also believe in God's goodness and mercy I found it hard to imagine that anyone would make such a final rejection. But that is God's business, not mine.

There will be a judgement, a final reckoning where we are brought face to face with God. On that day we will see ourselves as we really are and know ourselves in need of God's mercy. And we will see God as he truly is: we will look upon the face of love, and know God as the ultimate source of goodness and mercy. But on this side of heaven, we don't need to be afraid because the one who judges us is Jesus. And this judgement is the outpouring of reconciling love. Are we going to acknowledge our need and accept it is all that matters?

We are not being measured. Our goodness and our badness are not being weighed in the scales. If this were the case there would be no hope for anyone! Paul makes the point over and over again: it is by grace that we are saved, by God's free gift of his love and mercy.

Let us make this very clear: God wants us to enjoy eternal life with him; it is for this we are created. He will go to any lengths to save us. The God revealed to us in Jesus is the loving Father who runs out to meet his wayward children. He has faith in us and it is his faith – the faithful love of Jesus – that makes the difference. Through the cross, he has set aside the scales of justice and girded himself with the towel of service. We can therefore embrace grace and leave behind unhelpful and sadistic images of God presiding over the damnation of millions of lost souls, consigned to burn in hell. These damaging images of God have, in the past, turned Christianity into a religion of fear, and exchanged God's love for a rather nasty nepotism.

Judgement in John's Gospel is not God's decision about us, but our own choosing to reject God's way. Some of us do this again and again in life, refusing to change our ways, stubbornly avoiding all opportunities for forgiveness. And if we have 'loved darkness rather than light' (John 3:19), it is not that God has sent us to hell; rather, we have chosen to go there ourselves. Love has reached out to us, but we have decided to spit in love's face. 'Hell is not eternal torment, but it is the final irrevocable choosing of that which is opposed to God so completely and so absolutely that the only end is total non-being.'[8]

But because of what God has done in Jesus we can live our lives, not fearing judgement, but with an unconquerable hope that God's love and mercy *have* triumphed and *will* triumph. We have the great promise of heaven, and that, in Julian's famous phrase, 'all will be well'. God will gather together all the fragments of his creation and join us all in a unity of love: all of life will reflect and participate in the community of God, the life of the Trinity. As Paul puts it in one of the climactic passages of his letter to the Romans, nothing 'in all creation, will be able to separate us from the love of God in Christ Jesus our Lord' (Romans 8:39).

Failing to receive God's love is not the same as rejecting it. And many fail to receive God's love through no fault of their own. Often the church obscures and confounds God's message of love. Through it all God goes on loving those who reject him and hurt him and obstruct his way.

To accept God's love, however tentatively, indeed even to live in that love without ever knowing it, is to begin that process of being embraced by the cross of Christ, to begin to be transformed by his thirsting, searching love, to be made ready for heaven.

Julian of Norwich ends her account of the revelations she received with these words:

> From the time these things were first revealed I had often wanted to know what was our Lord's meaning. It was more than fifteen years after that I was answered in my spirit's understanding. 'You would know our Lord's mean-

ing in this thing? Know it well. Love was his meaning. Who showed it you? Love. What did it show you? Love. Why did it show it? For love. Hold on to this and you will know and understand love more and more. But you will not know or learn anything else – ever!' So it was that I learned that love was our Lord's meaning. And I saw for certain, both here and elsewhere, that before ever he made us, God loved us; and that his love has never slackened, nor ever shall. In this love all his works have been done, and in this love he has made everything serve us; and in this love our life is everlasting.[9]

And what of me? What does this say to me, as I try to make sense of the life given to me, of the time left to me? I stand before the cross and see Christ thirsting, and I am only too conscious of the many ways I have failed to be the person I am meant to be. These words 'I thirst' are the most intimate, the most personal and the most painful. For the greatest distress that Jesus suffered on the cross was not the nails, nor the spear, nor the scourging, nor the crown of thorns, but the rejection: our failure, and our continuing failure to show love. And in the revelation of God's great love I realize how trapped and compromised I am by my own sinfulness and self-centredness. I am the one who has failed to love. I am the one who has put self first. I am the one who has denied and rejected and betrayed. But in all this Jesus still loves me. He carries on loving me and will never stop loving me. He thirsts for me.

Implications for Today

What does it mean to love tenaciously? How does the knowledge that we are loved so completely change the way we think about ourselves and change the way we respond to others? The implications we are looking at in this chapter are all to do with how the example of Christ's tenacious love has guided and inspired others to love in the same way. In so doing, the true nature of love is discovered afresh. In particular, we will look at some individuals who have carried on loving against the odds. We will see how this kind of loving might affect two areas of our life. First, how we relate to people of other faiths (a difficult one for some Christians), and second, a personal one: how it affects human relationships.

The Lenten discipline we will explore is prayer. There is a great need for Christians' praying to be renewed. Understanding prayer as the way we receive the affirmation of God's love, the indwelling of the Holy Spirit drawing us into the community of God's own prayer, changes all our attitudes and relationships, enabling us to live and love like Christ. As we learn to receive from God, we will learn to give to others.

Tenacious loving

In his book *The Meaning in the Miracles* Jeffrey John contrasts what he calls 'the crusading mindset', sometimes prevalent in the more fanatical followers of all religions, with the crucified mindset, which is demonstrated on the cross. 'The crusading mind is rooted in intolerance, and its ultimate end is destruction of its opposition. The crucified mind is rooted in love which grows deeper through pain, and which seeks its end through what may seem a harsh and dreadful love, but whose aim is the transformation of its opponents.'[10]

In the cross we learn a way of loving that is tolerant, resolute and non-violent, a way of loving that will carry on expending itself no matter what opposition is placed in the way. The psalmist speaks of God's glory dwelling in the land in these words:

Mercy and truth are met together,
righteousness and peace have kissed each other. (Psalm 85:10[11])

So many of the conflicts that terrify our world arise from our inability to find a way of living that satisfies the twin demands of peace *and* justice. It always seems that one has to be sacrificed for the other to pertain. Anger and reprisal fuel and engulf so many human conflicts. Arguments for proportion and a desire for justice get overtaken by blood-lust and vengeance. 'There is no old age for a man's anger; only death,' wrote Sophocles many centuries ago. Indeed, the first great poem of world literature is about misplaced anger and its terrible consequences. Homer's *Iliad* begins, 'The wrath of Achilles is my theme, the fatal wrath which fulfilling Zeus's will, brought the Achaeans so much suffering, and sent many noble souls to Hades, leaving their bodies as carrion for vultures and dogs.'

From Homer's Greeks to our own day in Northern Ireland, Palestine, Israel, Iraq, and countless other places, we find ourselves crying out, 'Where do righteousness and peace kiss each other? How can mercy and truth embrace? How can we find a way of living that does not descend into the fatal cycle of retribution, terror and hurt?'

In the tenacity of Christ's love on the cross we see the dawning of fresh hope. On occasions too numerous to mention, the church has failed to preach and act with the same persistent love. I remember watching my children some years ago using the palm crosses, which they had received in church on Palm Sunday, as swords to fight each other under the pews. But isn't this just what the church has always done: turned the cross into a stick with which to beat people, used it to divide rather than unite the world? The church needs to repent of much. There are also bright moments of hope when the way of Christ has opened up a new way for the world. The many examples of godly, selfless individuals throughout history bring encouragement and hope. In them we see the tenacity of love at work.

In May 1963 Martin Luther King wrote this letter after the children's march, which campaigned against the unjust laws of racial segregation in the southern states of America:

> We must try to say to our white brothers all over the south who are trying to keep us down: We will match your capacity to inflict suffering with our capacity to endure suffering. We will meet your physical force with our soul force. We will not hate you. And yet we cannot in good conscience obey your evil laws. Do to us what you will. Threaten our children, and we will still love you ... We will wear you down by our capacity to suffer and still to love. In winning the victory we will truly win our freedom. We will so appeal to your heart and your conscience that we will win you in the process.[12]

This is a humbling example of tenacious, Christlike love, a love that longs to transform. We also know it was a love that triumphed, for the American Civil Rights movement eventually won great victories for oppressed black Americans. It was a love that suffered: through the privations and determination of many individuals, and, of course, through the shedding of Martin Luther King's own blood.

In the 1980s a similar response of non-violent love brought peaceful change to the Philippines. Not all has been well in that country since then, but that non-violence is still a marvellous example of love at work in the world. It seemed as if a massive electoral fraud would keep the oppressive President Marcos in power and lead to bloody civil war. But the election was won by Cory Aquino. In the years leading up to this a 'Fellowship of Reconciliation' had worked in the country, organizing retreats aimed at teaching people how to rely on the power of love and, with that power, to defeat the dictatorship. Many bishops and priests were involved in this work. Henri Nouwen writes about these events in the book he wrote for his nephew, *Letters to Marc about Jesus*:

> Cory Aquino's struggle against the dictatorship in her country was rooted in love for one's enemy. Before she presented herself as a candidate for the presidency, she prayed the whole night for her opponent, Ferdinand Marcos. She knew that hatred would lead to violence. The Filipino bishops and priests supported her and summoned the whole nation to non-violent resistance. When Marcos ordered out his tanks to crush his opponents, the soldiers refused to drive over the people who were praying. Priests wearing alb and stole approached the soldiers, embraced them, and invited them to drop their weapons and pray with the people for reconciliation and peace.[13]

And as we read this story many of us will remember the situation in China in the 1990s where students protested peacefully in Tiananmen Square for democracy and freedom. One of the remarkable images from those days is of a young man jousting, almost dancing, with a tank. But that protest was crushed violently. Sometimes that happens to love.

Neither is it only in the Christian tradition that we see the perseverance of love manifest in non-violent opposition. The example of Mahatma Gandhi is probably the most famous of the last century. Gandhi, and others like him, acted out of a deep belief in transforming love, that even evil is reversible and can be turned to good by the power of forgiveness. It is also true that one is best able to act in this transformative way if one is aware of one's own need to be transformed. It is precisely because we are aware of our own capacity for sin and violence, and of our need of God's grace and forgiveness, that we long to seek a peace where both oppressor and oppressed are liberated together. One cannot be free while the other is in chains.

In another, more recent example, the remarkably peaceful dismantling of apartheid in South Africa is a tribute to the resolute determination of many black people to oppose the terrible injustices of the system without necessarily demonizing all white people who supported it. Thus was born a 'rainbow people', not black dominance replacing white, but a transformation, a new way of living in harmony. Many moving moments and inspiring witnesses can be identified in the long struggle to bring freedom to black people in South Africa, such as the little story of Bishop Trevor Huddleston tipping his hat to a black woman: unheard of in apartheid South Africa, a small gesture of love returned to this woman a dignity and respect that her society had sought to take away. That woman was the mother of Desmond Tutu, who having witnessed the incident was given new heart for the struggle that lay ahead and new respect for the Christian church. He has spoken and written about the incident, and its significance, on many occasions.

Little gestures can make a big difference. In 1960, just a month after the Sharpeville massacre, David Sheppard, Bishop of Liverpool in the 1980s and 1990s, but then a priest and also an England cricketer, refused to captain the Duke of Norfolk's XI for the traditional match that started the South Africans' tour that year. He was the first test cricketer to make a public stand on this issue. It led to friction with many fellow-players, but now we can see that the sporting boycott of South Africa played a significant part in providing a peaceful way of telling the white people of South Africa that the rest of the world could not tolerate the injustices of their system.

But we cannot speak about the new South Africa without mentioning the tenacious loving of Nelson Mandela. Here are some of the final words he spoke at his trial. He did not contest the charges brought against him, for according to the unjust laws of apartheid he was indeed guilty, but used a plea of mitigation to speak for over an hour of the injustices that were being perpetrated on the black people of his country, and of how he was compelled to stand against them:

> I do not believe, Your Worship, that this court, in inflicting penalties on me for the crimes for which I am convicted should be moved by the belief that penalties will deter men from the course that they believe is right. History shows that penalties do not deter men when their conscience is aroused, nor will they deter my people or the colleagues with whom I have worked before . . .
>
> Whatever sentence Your Worship sees fit to impose upon me for the crime for which I have been convicted before this court, may it rest assured that when my sentence has been completed I will still be moved, as men are always moved, by their conscience; I will still be moved by my dislike of the race discrimination against my people when I come out from serving my sentence, to take up again, as best I can, the struggle for the removal of those injustices until they are finally abolished once and for all.[14]

There followed many years of imprisonment, and then the glorious dawning of freedom. Right at the end of his moving autobiography Mandela writes about the hope that sustained him:

I never lost hope that this great transformation would occur. Not only because of the great heroes I have already cited, but also because of the courage of the ordinary men and women of my country. I always knew that deep down in every human heart, there was mercy and generosity. No one is born hating another person because of the colour of his skin, or his background, or his religion. People must learn to hate, and if they can learn to hate, they can be taught to love, for love comes more naturally to the human heart than its opposite. Even in the grimmest times in prison, when my comrades and I were pushed to our limits, I would see a glimmer of humanity in one of the guards, perhaps just for a second, but it was enough to reassure me and keep me going . . .

It was during those long and lonely years that my hunger for the freedom of my own people became a hunger for the freedom of all people, white and black. I knew as well as I knew anything that the oppressor must be liberated just as surely as the oppressed. A man who takes away another man's freedom is a prisoner of hatred, he is locked behind bars of prejudice and narrow-mindedness. I am not truly free if I am taking away someone else's freedom, just as surely as I am not free when my freedom is taken from me. The oppressed and the oppressor are alike robbed of their humanity.

When I walked out of prison, that was my mission, to liberate the oppressed and the oppressor both.[15]

I could cite many other examples. Chad Varah, refusing to be defeated by the hopelessness of many suicides he ministered to as a young priest, set up the Samaritans as a way of extending love to those in deep despair and also transforming their situation. Dame Cicely Saunders, experiencing the inadequacy of so much care for the dying in the hospitals of Britain, resolved to find a new way of caring for those who were terminally ill. As founder of the modern Hospice Movement her readiness to go the second mile has brought comfort, relief and fresh hope in the face of death to countless thousands of people. Over and over again those who see the true power and beauty of love are compelled to strive in order for love and justice to triumph.

'Let love be genuine', says St Paul in the letter to the Romans; 'hate what is evil, hold fast to what is good' (Romans 12:9). 'Bless those who persecute you' (Romans 12:14). 'Do not repay anyone evil for evil' (Romans 12:17). 'Do not be overcome by evil, but overcome evil with good' (Romans 12:21).

All these examples witness to the overcoming of evil with good. Part of our vocation to live lives that reflect the life of Christ is to be 'overcomers'. When we face situations of injustice, be they large or small, our vocation is to pray for those who persecute us, to love those who oppose us, to seek a peace and reconciliation beyond the winning of an argument or the settling of a score. Our determined course must be the way of sacrificial loving. Only this will bring peace with justice.

Writing this in a world still confused and convulsed by the events of 11 September 2001, I have to ask, where is the witness of tenacious love? Have not too many of the responses of the West been born of vengeance, rather than love? While we rightly seek to bring to justice those who have perpetrated these terrible crimes against humanity, we need to work just as hard at building stability and trust with our Muslim neighbours in the Middle East who bear such grievances against us. Hardest of all, this will require of us a change of heart as we contemplate our own response to *receiving* pain. This is difficult to speak about. It seems too trite and easy to say that even when we have been the victims of terror we should carry on loving. I don't know whether I would be capable of this and, thank God, I have never been in such a position. But this is the way of Christ. All I can do is offer here two moving examples of those who have managed to respond to terror with love.

First, a Jewish prayer, the writer unknown, but found in the clothing of a dead child in the Ravensbruck concentration camp:

> Lord, remember not only the men and women of good will, but also those of ill will. But, do not remember all the suffering they have inflicted upon us: instead remember the fruits we have borne because of this suffering – our fellowship, our loyalty to one another, our humility, our courage, our generosity, the greatness of heart that has grown from this trouble. When our persecutors come to be judged by you, let all of these fruits that we have borne be their forgiveness.[16]

Second, is an astonishing prayer written by Hassan Dehqani-Tafti when he was the Anglican bishop in Iran after the murder of his son:

> O God we remember not only our son but also his murderers; not because they killed him in the prime of his youth and made our hearts bleed and our tears flow, not because with this savage act they have brought further disgrace on the name of our country among the civilized nations of the world; but because through their crime we are now to follow thy footsteps more closely in the way of sacrifice. The terrible fire of this calamity burns up all selfishness and possessiveness in us; its flame reveals the depth of depravity and meanness and suspicion, the dimension of hatred and the measure of sinfulness in human nature; it makes obvious as never before our need to trust in God's love as shown in the cross of Jesus and his resurrection; love which makes us free from hate towards our persecu-

tors; love which brings patience, forbearance, courage, loyalty, humility, generosity, greatness of heart; love which more than ever deepens our trust in God's final victory and his eternal designs for the Church and for the world; love which teaches us how to prepare ourselves to face our own day of death.

O God, our son's blood has multiplied the fruit of the Spirit in the soil of our souls; so when his murderers stand before thee on the day of judgement remember the fruit of the Spirit by which they have enriched our lives. And forgive.[17]

Prayer

The love we see poured out for us on the cross also affects our attitude to prayer. The knowledge that he loves us so completely, draws us into a relationship with God that should be marked by gratitude, adoration and a lack of inhibition. How can we not give thanks when we see the love of God expressed in Christ? How can our hearts not adore? How can we fail to bring all our concerns to the one who has made our life possible, who promises eternal life?

But what is prayer? My definition is this: prayer is the lover coming into the presence of the beloved, and saying, 'I love you'. And, of course, the lover is God. God is the one who is the author of life. God is the one who has made relationship possible. In Jesus he comes to us with outstretched arms. He lavishes his love upon us. He is the source of love. It is God who comes into our presence, searches us out, carries on loving even though we resist and ignore. He comes into our presence and says, 'I love you'.

We are the beloved, the object of God's love. We are the ones he longs to bring into the community of his love, which is his life in the Trinity. We are the ones he lives and dies for.

As in any relationship of love it is joy and delight to be in the presence of one's beloved. Thus does God have joy in us. It is sustained by the constant telling and retelling of the story of our love. Thus the Scriptures will always be shaping and informing our prayer. We need also to tell each other of our love. This, I suggest, is the foundation prayer: our hearing God's affirmation of love for us, and our responding with the same heartfelt desire. It is not looking for any reward. Yes, it is ready to bring to its beloved all its needs and cares. But most of all it is sufficient reward, and none other is sought, than to know that love is real.

Too often our understanding of prayer is shaped rather mechanistically. We might think of it as a way of changing God's mind – get enough signatures on the petition of prayer, and maybe God will act. Or we tell God what is happening in the world (as if he doesn't know!). Or else, if we do realize prayer is more than merely talking to God, we might think of it as filling up at a petrol station: our spiritual tank is approaching empty, so we pray, or go to church, or read a spiritual book. But even this, slightly better understanding of prayer is all need centred (I'll fill up when I'm empty) rather than love centred (I can do no other than be with my beloved). Prayer is first of all about what God says to us. It is about allowing ourselves to be changed and shaped by God's agenda for God's world. We come into the presence of God with thankful hearts for all he has done for us in Christ. We thank him for the gift of life – and this can happen anywhere and at any time. We still ourselves: we are in the presence of the one who loves us and we allow ourselves to hear his voice speaking his words of love. Sometimes we need the voice of God that speaks to us through the Bible, or through the liturgy of the church, to communicate this message of love. Or sometimes it is expressed to us through songs of praise. Sometimes we arrive at a place of complete silence, where it is sufficient just to know we are in God's presence. In each case we allow God to nurture within us, through his Holy Spirit, a deep sense of our being the beloved, of knowing we are loved. Then we can live and act with the same affirmation that sustained Christ, which enabled him to love others, which even made it possible for him to love his enemies. Only by knowing God's love for us, by knowing that we are worthy of his love, and therefore able to love ourselves more, can we reach out with love to others.

Another thing I remember from my childhood, which has sustained me through life, is my parents saying to me that if they lined up all the little boys in all the world, and walked up and down the line deciding which one to choose, they would choose me. The knowledge that I was their beloved, their chosen one, was a sure foundation for my life. It gave me freedom to become the person I was meant to be. It liberated me from imagining love had to be earned or deserved. And now I tell this same little tale of love to my own three children. I tell them that they are my chosen ones, my beloved. And I pray that this affirmation, the solid rock of unconditional love, will be a firm foundation for their lives. What is more, they now say the same thing back to me. They say that if they lined up all the dads in all the world they would choose me, that I am the best dad there is. And funnily enough the magic of their words still works: I feel the affirmation of their love. In a strange kind of way it works even better, because unlike them I know how undeserving I can be of that complete and unconditional loving. I know the many ways I have failed to be the dad I ought to be. But they love me not because of my achievements in fatherhood; they love me just because I am *their* dad, as I love them just because they are my children. This is how it is with God; this is the basis of the relationship we call 'prayer'.

In John's Gospel, on the night before he dies, Jesus says to his friends, 'You did not choose me, but I choose you' (John 15:16). You are my beloved – precious and beautiful in my sight. And I love you not because of your wit or wealth or wisdom; I love you just because you are.

In a world that still wants to evaluate people by what they have achieved or what they earn or what they wear, this is powerful good news. You are loved and precious in the eyes of God just because you are.

Consequently, there is no such thing as private prayer. Prayer always unites us to the God who is Trinity: a community of love. God's invitation is that we might participate in this life. Prayer empties us of self-obsession. Instead, learning an authentic self-love, we also have a deep sense of our own belonging to each other. We realize that we have all fallen short of what God intends. We discover a transparency of living where we no longer need to pretend to be the good people we have supposed ourselves to be (or that we have hoped others might think us to be). We can just be ourselves: loved by God, loving ourselves, and now able to love our neighbours.

Lent is a time when we are called to deepen our life of prayer. As we have seen, this is less about techniques and more about attitudes. Taking hold of the certainty, the irresistibility, the tenacity of God's love, we live the rest of our lives in response. Simply saying 'I love you' back to God is the greatest prayer of all.

It may be that you will need to talk to someone about your life of prayer. The longer you have been a member of the church the harder it gets to admit that you find prayer difficult. But take courage: you are not alone. There are, I am afraid, many Christians who do not pray. Indeed, as I have written elsewhere, I can best describe myself when it comes to prayer as an experienced beginner!

Change comes when we find within ourselves a *desire* to pray. (Seeing clearly the love of God in Christ is surely the beginning of this.) And by nurturing a *discipline* of prayer. And here we will need the help of others: people to pray with, and help in finding the way of praying that suits us best. Our prayer will find different expressions according to our temperament, personality and circumstances.[18]

Finally we need to realize that prayer itself is the work of God. It is not we who pray, but the Holy Spirit praying within us. Our prayer is united with the prayer of Jesus to the Father, and we are drawn ever closer to the joys of life lived fully in communion with God. This means we can relax. There is no need to try too hard. We find the way of praying that is right for us, and we allow moments of prayer and specific times of prayer to punctuate our daily lives. In this way we become prayerful, loving people.

With this in mind – especially the specific challenge of Jesus to love our enemies and pray for those who persecute us – let me briefly mention two other implications that arise from these reflections. They both affect our relationships with others.

Generous particularity

One of the great challenges facing the world in the twenty-first century is the relationship between different religions. It is all too easy to make ourselves judge, dividing the world into those who have responded to the love of God in Christ and those who haven't. Clearly, so this kind of logic goes, people of other faiths are on the wrong side of the divide. What can we say to this situation, while still maintaining the particular and definitive revelation of God's love in the cross of Christ?

Jesus himself had an irritating habit of jumping over all the boundaries set up around the Jewish notions of righteousness with God. For instance, he makes a hated and heretical Samaritan the hero of his story about who is a neighbour (we will look more at this in a later chapter); he gives way to the Syro-Phoenician woman, commending her faith; he heals the Roman centurion's friend; he regularly eats with tax collectors and prostitutes. In fact, one could argue that the only people Jesus is quick to judge are those who are quick to judge others.

The vocation to love our neighbour is not superseded by the commission to share the gospel. We must be true to our calling to share good news of what God has done in Christ, but we must do it in the *manner and style* of Christ, leaving matters of judgement to him.

We also do well to remember that in all likelihood Jesus never intended to start a new religion. Jesus saw his mission to *fulfil* Judaism, not to divide it. The first tragedy of Christian history is the early schism with Judaism, and from that the shameful anti-Semitism that has polluted some Christian witness, and has even found its way into some parts of the New Testament.

What Jesus actually models for us, what he seeks to achieve in himself, is the fulfilment of *all* religious longing and desire for God. Therefore the first Christians were also Jews, seeing no contradiction between their Judaism and their faith in Christ. Theological challenges lay ahead – such as, should Gentile converts to the way of Christ, baptized into the new covenant, also have to be circumcised and thereby be admitted to the old covenant? But never was this intended as disrespectful or unheeding of what God had done through his people Israel.

In our relationships with people of other faiths we should affirm what is good and holy in their religion. There is no problem about us working together to secure common regard for faith, and uniting on various issues of justice and relief for the poor. But there is also no point in pretending all religions are the same. The revelation of God in Jesus Christ is disturbingly particular. What we know about God through Christ is given for the whole world to know. Therefore, there will be times when we will quietly need to take a stand on the truth of our faith as we have received it. But in my experience of living and working in two parts of Britain where there are a great many people of other faiths, they are often more surprised by a Christian's reluctance to talk about faith than his or her insistence upon it.

Our motivation must be love. We share the gospel because we know God to be our lover, and we share it with everybody, regardless of what other beliefs they may or may not hold. We share it because we know that God's love in Christ can set us free from fear and sin. We share it, not coercively or judgementally, but in a way consistent with love, because to do otherwise would be a denial of the very message we proclaim. Christian witness should always be gentle, humble, tolerant and respectful. When people of other faiths do come to follow the way of Christ they will bring with them all that was good from their previous faith tradition. When they don't, we simply carry on loving, carry on rejoicing in all that is good in their lives and their religion, carry on persistently witnessing to our own faith through the lives we lead and through the witness we humbly share. We approach people of other faiths in a way that is true to our own faith.

But there is also an important theological issue here about who will be saved. The New Testament tells us that we will be surprised by who God calls to life eternal. As was said earlier, the realities of love demand that we reject a blanket universalism. It cannot simply be that all will enjoy life with God, for all are free to accept or reject God's love. Though we may find it hard to conceive of such ultimate rejection of God, this in the end is not for us to know or judge. Logic requires us to concede that some people, so poisoned by their own wrong choices here on earth, will continue to confound the purposes of God and never accept his love. But this does not mean God ever stops loving them.

Similarly, we must reject a rigid, unloving exclusivism, making ourselves judge of who is and who isn't enjoying God's favour. It is God's love and mercy that saves, not the categories of blessedness we construct. Therefore, there may be people whom we think will be the last here on earth, but to our surprise will actually be first in the kingdom of heaven.

Human relationships

Another area of our life that would benefit from the kind of loving Jesus shows us is our close relationships with each other, especially in the family. Here is something really worth giving up for Lent. Husbands and wives, lovers and friends, give up being so short-tempered and intolerant with each other. Parents give up failing to listen to your children. Instead, let us resolve to go the second mile in our relationships with those who are our nearest and dearest. Love needs time and patience to prosper and bear fruit.

The love of Christ shows us that it is only when we have persisted that we will know true love. What does this mean for our marriages, our relationships and our families? How often have we not just neglected one another, but given up at the very point that real love, beyond the instant gratification of infatuation and desire, was opening up as a possibility in our lives. To be sure, this was a love that may only have been attained through some suffering, and would also have involved painful self-examination and resolute determination. But it was the possibility of a beautiful love, a love that truly reflected the love of God – and it was lost to us. Lost, because we had allowed ourselves to be seduced by something else: something we call love, but something that, in fact, was an illusion, a quick fix, an addiction to *feeling* loved, rather than the tough road of *actually* loving.

This does not mean that all breakdowns in relationships and marriages should have been avoided; life is never that simple. But it does mean that if we are to find in human relationships the fulfilment we crave, we must recognize our addiction to the superficiality of so much that passes for love, and determine to work harder and love more tenaciously in the relationships that lie before us. Perhaps it would be better if, like the Greek language, the English language had more than one word for love. It would force us to differentiate between passing fancy and committed love. It would help us to aspire to a love like God's love for us.

Final Thought

What is the most radical and subversive verse in the Bible? Surely it is this: 'Love your enemies' (Matthew 5:43). Or, as Paul puts it, 'if your enemies are . . . thirsty, give them something to drink' (Romans 12:20). This is the disturbing topsy-turvy message of the New Testament, an affront to good taste, a political platform that will win no votes: reach out to your enemies in love. Quench the thirst of those who disagree with you and oppose you in the same way that God has quenched your thirst in Christ. If we want peace in the world (rather than just our own security), there is no other way. It is love for enemies as well as friends that marks out the Christian life.

For Discussion

Reflecting on God's Word

1 Read aloud Romans 12:9–21.

2 Spend some time in silence.

3 Invite people to speak aloud into the silence a word or phrase that strikes them from the passage.

4 In pairs or small groups share with each other the words and phrases that have been spoken and how they help you to consider what it means in your situation to 'love tenaciously'?

Deepening our Understanding of Lent

1 As we consider the tenacity of God's love as revealed on the cross, what are the implications for our relationships
   • in the church community?
   • in our homes and families?
   • with people of other faiths?
   • with those we would think of as our enemies?

Perhaps split into groups to discuss these different areas and then share conclusions and reflections.

1 How does our church help people to grow in prayer? What more needs to be done?

2 How is God challenging us to be the answer to our own prayers? In other words, in the light of all our exploration and discussion thus far, how is God calling us to get involved in actually showing love to others in those areas where we have need or concern?

3 How has the phrase 'the tenacity of love' helped us to understand what is happening on the cross?

For Reflection

Although I am dust and ashes, Lord, I am tied to you by bonds of love. Therefore I feel I can speak freely to you. Before I came to know you, I was nothing. I did not know the meaning of life, and I had no understanding of myself. I have no doubt that you had a purpose in causing me to born; yet you had no need of me, and on my own I was of no use to you. But then you decided that I should hear the words of your Son, Jesus Christ. And that as I heard his words, you enabled his love to penetrate my heart. Now I am completely saturated in his love and faith, and there is no remedy. Now, Lord, I cannot change attitude to my faith; I can only die for it.[19]

Jesus proclaimed that in being lifted up he would draw all to himself. In his cry 'I am thirsty', the energy that exerts itself upon us, the current that pulls us towards him in spite of our doubt and resistance, the undertow that carries us off our feet when we want to halt a distance away, is revealed as divine eros, God's thirst to bring us into union with himself.[20]

For Prayer

Dear Lord, it seems that you are so madly in love with your creatures that you could not live without us. So you created us; and then, when we turned away from you, you redeemed us. Yet you are God, and so have no need of us. Your greatness is made no greater by our creation; your power is made no stronger by our redemption. You have no duty to care for us, no debt to repay us. It is love, and love alone, which moves you.[21]

CHAPTER 5

Enduring Thirst

Come, you that are blessed by my father, inherit the kingdom prepared for you from the foundation of the world; for I was hungry and you gave me food, I was thirsty and you gave me something to drink.

MATTHEW 25:34–35

I can recall only one time in my life when I have been really thirsty. Many years ago, before we were married, my wife and I travelled by coach from London to the south of France. The coach left Victoria Station at about eight in the evening, and we travelled all through the night, arriving near Toulon the following morning. We had not prepared well for the journey, and I don't think we had any water with us. Or if we did, it was consumed early on. The coach didn't have any air conditioning and it was a very hot, sticky night. In the small hours of the morning I can remember feeling desperate for a drink of water. I expect I had drunk some red wine on the ferry, and the dehydrating effects of the alcohol probably accentuated the longing of my thirst.

At about five in the morning we stopped at a service station on the AutoRoute. We were all allowed out to stretch our legs and visit the shop. There was only one thing I wanted – water. It was a desperate kind of thirst. I had never experienced anything like it, nor have I since.

There are two things I particularly remember. I remember first that, going into the shop, just seeing the bottles of water on the refrigerator shelf was itself a huge relief. It brought the knowledge that my aching thirst would soon be quenched. There was joy even in the anticipation of a drink. Then there was drinking the water itself. It was ice cold, and as I gulped it down I felt my whole body refreshed, as if it were being irrigated, brought back to life. It was a feeling of such immense satisfaction that I can easily remember it even now, and have often recalled it over the years. And yet the suffering I endured, for what was only a few hours on that coach, is minuscule compared with the suffering of Christ, and almost insulting to mention when compared with the unquenched thirst of so many thousands and millions of people across our world today. I mention this incident, not because I really suffered from it, but to try to describe the joy that comes when such a burning thirst is slaked.

As we behold Christ upon the cross, as in our imaginations we look at him turned on a griddle of suffering, aching, parched, lonely, we behold someone whose whole body is raging with a terrible thirst. Pain wracks his dehydrated body. A deep longing for God and a profound compassion for the world wells up in his soul. As he dies, the soldiers give him a drink, and he is happy to receive it from them. If – and I believe this is the correct reading of the incident – the *posca* is offered to Jesus by the soldiers as an act of mercy, he receives their kindness gratefully. Yet these are still the people who have nailed him to the cross, carrying out their grim orders. But they have also received from him. Jesus has shown them mercy: 'Father forgive them' were the words of generous love Jesus spoke to his executioners. Perhaps this has released mercy and compassion within them.

This beautiful exchange of mercy, whereby love triumphs and multiplies, is what I call in this book the tenacity of love. In Jesus the dogged persistence of God's love is poured out for us. In this sense we will always know him as the one who is thirsty – thirsting in pain, thirsting with compassion. It would, therefore, be a mistake to see the thirsting of Jesus on the cross as something that happened once at Calvary and is now finished. Because the cross reveals the nature of God as love, the cross stands forever as a sign of God's passionate involvement in the world. In John's Gospel the risen Christ still bears the marks of suffering (see John 20:20). There is, therefore, a real sense in which Christ is still thirsty today. We encounter him in all situations where there is pain and want. We see him on the cross in the suffering of the world, and we hear him cry out in thirst. Therefore, our response to him involves much more than the eloquence of our faith. It is not just a matter of believing in Christ; it is about serving Christ in the thirst of the world. 'Have we given him a drink?' is the sobering question we need to ask ourselves.

When did we see you thirsty?

In St Matthew's Gospel, just before the beginning of the passion narrative, there are three parables, all of which deal with the theme of judgement. First, Jesus tells the story of the ten bridesmaids, five who are foolish and have no oil to replenish their lamps, and five who are wise, with oil to spare, and are therefore ready when the bridegroom comes.

Then there is the story of the talents: different sums of money are given to some slaves according to their different abilities. When the master returns from a long journey the slaves are held to account; most have made some profit on the original sum they were given, but one slave has simply hidden his talent in the ground and made nothing. He is reprimanded for his wastefulness, and even the one talent he has is taken from him and given to another.

Finally, Jesus offers a picture of the Son of Man coming in glory and gathering the nations before him for judgement, as a shepherd divides sheep from goats. The King says to those on his right hand that they will receive the inheritance of God's kingdom promised from the foundation of the world. These are the ones who fed the King when he was hungry, who quenched his thirst when he was thirsty, who welcomed him when he came to them as a stranger, who clothed him when he was naked, who took care of him when he was sick, and who visited him when he was in prison. They are mystified: 'Lord, when was it that we saw you hungry and gave you food, or thirsty and gave you something to drink?' (Matthew 25:37). 'When you did it to the least of these, my brothers and sisters, you did it to me' (Matthew 25:40[1]) replies the King.

At this, those on the King's left hand – who have been separated from the righteous – respond with indignation: 'Lord, when was it that we saw you hungry or thirsty or a stranger or naked or sick or in prison, and did not take care of you?' (Matthew 25:44). For them the King's reply is devastating: 'just as you did not do it to one of the least of these, you did not do it to me' (Matthew 25:45).

Here Jesus sets out the criterion by which the nations will be judged: compassion. It is by our love and care for others that we will be judged. In ministering to them, we will minister to Christ. We will not necessarily realize it is Christ, and, in a way, this does not matter: the righteous who inherit the kingdom have not asked questions about the status of the person in need; they have simply done what love and compassion demand. They have carried on loving, regardless of who it is and of how futile the gesture might seem to others. They have carried on loving even if they did not feel very loving. Hence they are surprised by the reward they receive.

They did not love because it was Christ; they did not love because they were looking for a reward: they loved in response to the need they encountered. And even if they did not realize it themselves, they loved because of the love they had received, an overflowing of the grace that comes from being loved, an inner compulsion that is itself a reflection of God. 'We love, because he [God] first loved us' (1 John 4:19). Here again we see the beautiful dynamic of the gospel unfolding before us in the drama of the cross, and lived out in the lives of many people, both those who have consciously responded to Christ, and also in those of other beliefs and religions who, while not yet knowing Christ, live lives of self-forgetful loving.

On the other hand, there are those who have not loved. They are equally surprised. They do not feel they have actually done anything wrong. Indeed, they may be the very religious people who have been so scrupulous in their observance of their religion's requirements and demands. But they have not taken care of those in need. It is not that one group recognized Christ and the other did not. It is simply that one group showed compassion.

Henri Nouwen makes this observation in an article he wrote about the second coming of Christ:

> Our lives as we live them seem like lives that anticipate questions that will never be asked. It seems as if we are getting ourselves ready for the question 'How much did you earn during your lifetime?' or 'How many friends did you make?' or 'How much progress did you make in your career?' or 'How much influence did you have?' . . . or 'How

many conversions did you make?' ... but nobody is going to hear any of these questions. The question we are all going to face is the question we are least prepared for. It is the question 'What have you done for the least of mine?'[2]

The tragedy for those who are placed on God's left hand is that they have somehow missed the whole point of life. They have lived their lives pursuing goals that were either secondary to the primary purposes of God, or were sometimes unwittingly at odds with God. Hence, they have ignored Christ when he was in need. In seeking to preserve themselves, and gain the whole world, they end up losing their soul. Why? Because those who cry out in thirst have remained thirsty. And in them Christ still hangs upon the cross; he still cries out.

There is a link here with the other parables of judgement. The parable of the wise and foolish bridesmaids alerts us to the urgency of the situation. We cannot put off the need to respond to the love God shows us in Christ, for we do not know the hour of judgement. The parable of the talents reminds us that we have to live out this vocation of love within the difficult realities of our world as it is. Therefore, it is not wrong to pursue other goals. It is not wrong, for instance, to work hard to pass examinations, to want careers that will satisfy, nor even to expect some material benefit for the work we do. It is just that in the end our lives will not be measured by these criteria. It is not about how much money we earned, or what jobs we had. Neither, I stress again, is it about the depth or efficacy of our faith. Rather, it is about how we have used our gifts. How have we used the faith, the money, the opportunities, the time we received? Have we used them only for our own well-being, or have we offered them in thanksgiving to God and deployed them in the service of all humanity?

This is an uncomfortable question for all Christian people to face. Often, rather than face up to what it means to work out our discipleship in the world as it is, we prefer to fantasize about giving up everything to follow Christ. Because it is unlikely that most of us will receive this call to a life of poverty we avoid asking how we will actually use the time and gifts we have been given. Perhaps it is hard to face this question because the answers are invariably quite easy to identify. Most of us know there is lots more we could be doing if we ordered the priorities of our life in different ways. It is putting it into action that is hard.

Becoming thirsty

There is, however, another, and for Western ears more radical, way of reading this parable of judgement. I was made aware of this interpretation some years ago while listening to the witness and experience of African Christians who were working as mission partners with me in the Wakefield diocese as part of a Church Missionary Society exchange programme.

In an earlier episode in Matthew's Gospel, Jesus says to his disciples, 'Whoever welcomes you welcomes me, and whoever welcomes me welcomes the one who sent me . . . and whoever gives even a cup of cold water to one of these little ones in the name of a disciple – truly I tell you, none of these will lose their reward' (Matthew 10:40,42).

Here the reward seems to be promised to those who in welcoming a disciple welcome Christ. The implication seems to be that it is the disciples who are the thirsty ones who will be ministered to, and those who are compassionate towards them will not be forgotten. Mark's version of this saying of Jesus makes the point even more explicitly: 'For truly I tell you, whoever gives you a cup of water to drink because you bear the name of Christ will by no means lose the reward' (Mark 9:41).

What surprised my Western ears when listening to those African Christians read the Bible, was that it never occurred to them to identify with anyone in the story other than those who were thirsty. They saw their discipleship of Christ necessarily involving them in a witness that would involve all those things Matthew lists in the parable with which we began this chapter. They would be hungry, they would be thirsty, they would become strangers, they would be naked, they would be imprisoned. This was both their experience of the Christian life and their expectation. And, of course, this was the experience of the first Christian communities. Writing to the church in Corinth, Paul says that 'To the present hour we are hungry and thirsty, we are poorly clothed and beaten and homeless, and we grow weary from the work of our own hands' (1 Corinthians 4:11–12a). He then goes on to describe again the attitude of tenacious love: 'When reviled, we bless; when persecuted, we endure; when slandered, we speak kindly' (1 Corinthians 4:12b–13a). And in a beautiful passage in the second letter to the Corinthians Paul says this:

> as servants of God we have commended ourselves in every way: through great endurance, in afflictions, hardships, calamities, beatings, imprisonments, riots, labours, sleepless nights, hunger; by purity, knowledge, patience, kindness, holiness of spirit, genuine love, truthful speech, and the power of God; with the weapons of righteousness for the right hand and for the left; in honour and dishonour, in ill repute and good repute. We are treated as impostors, and yet are true; as unknown, and yet are well known; as dying, and see – we are alive; as punished, and yet not killed; as sorrowful, yet always rejoicing; as poor, yet making many rich; as having nothing, and yet possessing everything. (2 Corinthians 6:4–10)

It seemed that these African Christians knew what this meant, not just from their reading of the Bible, but from their everyday experience of living the Christian life. However, when we read the story of the sheep and the goats in the affluent West we do not associate ourselves with the thirsty, but with those who have water to offer. We feel much more comfortable being the ones who are able to give, rather than the ones who are forced to receive. Many of us will never have seriously considered that following Christ may bring us to a point where we need charity from others. Whereas in the West we see ourselves as the ones who provide for Christ, in Africa they are those in whom Christ, the thirsty one, can be encountered.

Again, I must confess to finding myself on the edge of my own experience of the gospel. For I have never really suffered for my faith. I have never really been hungry or thirsty or in serious need. Yes, there have been times when I have been vulnerable and received the ministry of others, but most of the time I have been the one in control; and I have been the one who had gifts, resources and time to offer. I, therefore, find it hard to imagine being in a place of poverty, still less finding the compulsion of the gospel taking me to a place of poverty. And again I realize how compromising and difficult it is to live out the Christian vocation in a seductive culture like ours. I take some small solace from the fact that it is good at least to acknowledge the difficulty we are in.

Both interpretations of the story have important things to say. It is not that it is wrong to associate ourselves with the generosity of those who in ministering to the needy minister to Christ – how could it be otherwise, when we live in a society with such plenty? But there is a challenge for us about how we use and share our resources. How do we find a just and equitable way of distributing the world's resources? How do we live with the same bias to the poor, the marginalized, the suffering that was such a feature of Jesus' ministry?

These are hard questions to face. Harder still is the suggestion that if we are following Christ, then he will take us to places where others will need to minister to us, and in doing this they will find their salvation because, unknowingly, they will be quenching Christ's thirst. In discovering what it really means to imitate the Christ who is thirsty, we may need to free ourselves from the comfortable security of always being the ones who can give, but forgetting how to receive.

The least of these

A further interpretation of this story touches powerfully upon the way we treat the whole created order, particularly our fellow-creatures. 'The least of these' can refer to animals abused and exploited in so many atrocious ways. The food scares that have rocked our world in recent years have invariably arisen directly from the appalling ill treatment of animals in our gluttonous desire to have cheap meat on our tables every day. Then there are the unnecessary cruelties of much animal experimentation. 'The least of these' can be the species facing extinction because of the destruction of their natural habitats. 'The least of these' can be the fauna and flora themselves disappearing as land turns to desert, as rainforests are plundered and polluted. Our attitude to the creation of which we are a part is a vital issue for Christians today. We need to find ways of preventing the planet itself from overheating in the cauldron of our misuse. We need to find ways of preserving and cherishing the fragile equilibrium of our planet's life and the multi-faceted beauty of its many creatures.

A recent report from the Washington-based Worldwatch Institute reckoned that the human race had only one or perhaps two generations to rescue itself.[3] Global warming is accelerating, toxic chemicals are being released in ever increasing quantities, global production of hazardous wastes continues to rise, and we have only the vaguest ideas of what the long-term effects of all this will be. All we know is that things are getting worse. 1.2 billion people – a fifth of the world's population – live in absolute poverty, but populations continue to grow. Of the world's surviving rain-forests 30 per cent are seriously fragmented or degraded and are still being cut down at a rate of around 130,000 square kilometres (50,000 square miles) a year. Wetlands have been reduced by 50 per cent in a century. Coral reefs are being destroyed. The ice caps are melting and sea levels rising. A quarter of the world's mammals and 12 per cent of the birds are in danger of extinction. Huge problems face our planet – most of them created by the choices a few of us have made about how we wish to order the world. As stewards of God's creation we have to do something to care for those who have no power to speak for themselves. How many deaths, how many extinctions, will it take before we listen to the cry of a thirsty world? Indeed, all the reports reckon that the greatest threat of all for life on this planet is a shortage of water.

Implications for Today

The implications we are going to look at in this chapter are all connected with the Lenten discipline of almsgiving. Giving is not just about money; it is about a whole attitude to life, to all our possessions, our time and our gifts.

We will look first at the severe water shortages that cripple the earth and think how we might contribute towards changing this situation. We will also touch on some of the other global and environmental issues that Christians ought to be more concerned about. Finally, we will explore how we might respond to some of the real needs of real people we encounter in the course of our daily lives.

Slaking the world's thirst

If you go to the website of WaterAid – a UK charity dedicated exclusively to the provision of water, sanitation and the promotion of hygiene among the world's poorest people – you will find both interesting and startling statistics. Did you know, for instance, that a human being requires 2.5 litres (4 pints) of water for drinking and 9 litres (16 pints) for hygiene each day? That is 11.5 litres (20 pints) altogether. Yet in Britain we use 80 litres (141 pints) of water every time we run a bath, 35 litres (62 pints) every time we take a shower or use the dishwasher, 10 litres (18 pints) every time we flush the toilet. And if you consider how many times each day a toilet is flushed you will not be surprised to learn the grim statistic that a third of the water used each day by a family in Britain is flushed down the lavatory. In fact, the average Briton uses 135 litres (238 pints) of water each day, enough for 12 people. If we compare usage in the United States this figure soars to a staggering 500 litres (880 pints) per person. Yet even this pales against the amount of water the manufacturing industry uses: over 113,650 litres (25,000 gallons) of water needed to make just *one car*!

And yet, against this, a quarter of the world's population is without safe drinking water. Every 8 seconds a child in the developing world dies from a disease unsafe water causes. This is the equivalent of the number of passengers that would die if about 20 Jumbo jets crashed every day.[4] Yet this appalling, and quite easily avoidable, statistic is not the headline in the newspapers every day. We have our minds on other things.

We inhabit a parched world, but as long as there is water in our tap we think little of the thirst of others. Although water is for many a scarce commodity, as ever the rich have a lot more than their fair share.

It would be complacent, however, to imagine that water shortage is just a developing-world issue. The problems concerning the availability of fresh water are at their most severe in the developing world, but the rest of us are also affected. The global consumption of fresh water doubles every 20 years and new sources are becoming scarcer and more expensive to develop and treat. As the world develops and populations increase, countries suffering serious water scarcity also increase. Most of Africa, the Middle East and South Asia are already in trouble. But so are the western United States, South America, China and nearly all of Australia. Some 70 per cent of all the world's fresh water is used to grow food, and we will need more food and more water as the world population expands.

We are also using up the water stored in underground reservoirs. A quarter of the world's population gets its supplies from aquifers, deep underground supplies of water. But these are mined ten times faster than they are naturally recharged. In parts of China, water tables are dropping almost 1.5 metres (5 feet) a year. In Tamil Nadu, in India, they have dropped 30 metres (98 feet) in 30 years and many aquifers have run dry. The ecological consequences of this are also overlooked. Deep aquifers, which are part of the hydrological cycle, release water slowly into rivers in the dry seasons and soak up water in the wet ones. The reason why many of the world's great rivers flow all year round is because of this water released from deep under the ground. Without it the rivers would run dry. Elsewhere in the industrialized world aquifers have been polluted by pesticides, nitrates, petrochemicals and other waste products. Many people are drinking poisoned water and are hardly aware of it. Deforestation also contributes to the cycles of climatic change that create droughts followed by floods.

We are not yet at the stage where nations will be at war with one another over the supply and availability of water, but we are not far from it. Wealthy, food-producing countries compete for a finite resource.

But, of course, the situation is worst for the poor. This is how Pat Ashworth, writing in the *Church Times*, describes the situation of the poor:

> The familiar image of the remote African or Asian village in which women spend the bulk of each day collecting water from sources several kilometres away is still true in many places. In Sierra Leone, for example, it is estimated that nine-year-old girls spend six hours a day on water-related activities. But as much, or even more, of a challenge are the marginalized areas around the big cities and provincial towns to which the world's poorest people move to get work. They find themselves living in shanty towns with no water or sanitation, and paying exorbitant prices for low-quality, dirty water from private vendors.[5]

The price the poor pay is much more, however, than the wicked inflated prices. In Surat in India in 1995 an epidemic of pneumonic plague broke out because the rotting carcasses of livestock were washed into the water system after heavy monsoon floods. Cholera returned to Latin America in the 1990s for the first time in a hundred years.

'Lord, when did we see you thirsty' is the question we face. The answer screams at us as we encounter the thirsty Christ in the thirsty people of the world. Recognizing this has implications large and small for how we conduct our lives.

First, we need to take more seriously the global and environmental issues concerning poverty and the supply of fresh water. We need to be more ready to embrace the change needed to secure fresh water for ourselves and provide the developing world with the fresh water it so desperately requires. Perhaps we should be less critical of being charged for our own use of water. At least it ensures that much less water is wasted, thus aiding conservation.

There needs to be more aid, and also more focused aid, concentrating on the needs of smaller, local communities. This has been the thrust of WaterAid's work and a story from their website illustrates the difference such a small community-focused project can make, especially where the local community is involved in every step of the planning so that it meets their needs and priorities.

Lucy Akanboguure tells the story of what happened in her village of Kandinga, in Ghana, where her community suffered from severe water shortages during the long dry season, from November to March. The scarcity of water meant people spent many hours each day journeying to a nearby river to collect it. This in turn led to much fighting and quarrelling in the village. Often water was so scarce that the villagers were forced to collect dirty water, which posed terrible health hazards. Sanitary facilities were generally non-existent. Diarrhoea, dysentery, guinea-worm and cholera were rife, and often resulted in death because there were no adequate health facilities. All the children in the neighbourhood were severely malnourished.

Hearing about WaterAid's work, Lucy organized the community and asked for assistance. In 1995, after several meetings, the project was agreed, and the first of two hand-dug wells were constructed as part of a joint project between the village and WaterAid, both parties contributing labour, funding and expertise. Lucy takes up the story in her own words:

> On the first day after the handpump was installed, I woke up at 6 a.m., and cried aloud, thinking I was too late to fetch water from the river. Then I realized that, in their excitement, my children had woken up earlier and filled the water pots with clean water, and were already preparing breakfast. I felt so happy having water at my doorstep, 24 hours a day, knowing that I was safe from water diseases.[6]

This is another story that ends in joy as water is provided and thirst is quenched. But there is more we could be doing – and water is not the only issue that concerns the world. There is an interrelatedness between the political choices we make, the lifestyles we pursue, and the state of the planet we inhabit. The more we plunder and abuse the resources of the planet, and the more we disregard the needs of the developing world, the more we store up environmental, economic and political problems.

Often we feel powerless in the face of these huge, global issues. It all seems too much. This leads to a kind of inertia. We imagine that these problems do not really exist, or are not as bad as the do-gooders and scaremongers make out. Or, more commonly, we carry on living and acting as if they don't exist. So we know, for instance, that we can buy fairly traded goods from Oxfam or Christian Aid, but we don't; we know we can recycle a lot more of our household waste, but we never actually get round to doing it. Without considering what we can do ourselves, we harp on about the government's failings. We have stopped believing that our contribution can make a difference.

If the Christian faith teaches us anything, it teaches us that one person can move mountains. Supremely this is so in the case of Jesus himself: he has made a huge difference to the world. But if you find him too demanding a role model, look at the lives of those men and women the church calls the 'saints'. These are people who have opened themselves up to God's grace and energy and have changed the world. Mary's yes to God made a massive difference. The first disciples, most of them illiterate and uneducated fishermen, made a difference. Or think of people like those we discussed in the last chapter: Nelson Mandela, Cicely Saunders or Trevor Huddleston. Or think of the little people, whose witness is known only to God, and maybe a handful of others: that Chinese student waving down a tank, or those who have written to Amnesty International or given to support the work of Christian Aid or WaterAid or Oxfam, or got involved in the local community. All through the ages individual men and women have seized God's agenda for the world, sought to make it real in their own lives, lived it with passion and vigour and as a result wrought great changes.

One of the most urgent needs the human race faces is how we safeguard the integrity of God's creation. I like the story of the teenager who berates her parents and their generation for ruining the world and the environment. 'Well, if you want to clean up the world', replies the weary parent, 'you can begin with your bedroom.' In one way this could be read as a cynical response. In another it reveals an important truth. Yes, there are big global and international issues we must face, but there are also, smaller things, closer to home, we can do, and often it is in doing the small things that energy for the bigger issues is found. Actually doing something, however small, keeps the big issues on the agenda and does in itself make a difference somewhere. What may seem like a drop in the ocean to us, is a life-saving drink of water to the thirsty person.

Here are twelve practical things many of us could do, which would make a difference.[7]

1 *Start a compost heap* to reduce the waste you send to landfill sites.

2 *Slow down.* Driving at 80 kilometres (50 miles) per hour uses 25 per cent less fuel than 113 kilometres (70 miles) per hour.

3 *Turn down your central heating* and put on a jumper.

4 *Take a brisk shower* rather than a leisurely bath.

5 *Buy compact fluorescent light bulbs.* They last eight times as long and use a fraction of the energy.

6 *Get on your bike* – or walk – instead of driving.

7 *Use low-phosphate washing-up liquid and washing powder.* Phosphates stimulate algal growth when discharged into the water supply, lowering oxygen levels and killing plants and fish.

8 *Use recycling facilities.*

9 *Refuse plastic carrier bags,* or at least reuse them.

10 *Invest in a washing line:* tumble-driers devour electricity.

11 *Bring a mug to the office* instead of using polystyrene cups.

12 *Only flush toilets when it is really necessary.* The Australians have a graphic saying: 'If it's yellow that's mellow; if it's brown flush it down!' Much

to my three sons' pleasure and amusement we are successfully piloting this scheme in my own household. For years we ticked them off if they didn't pull the chain; now we tick them off if they do! Or, if you find this too disgusting to contemplate, just put a brick in the cistern. This will save some of the water you usually flush away.

These are all relatively small lifestyle changes that would cost nothing: in fact, they would save money as well as helping to save the planet. But there are other things – such as buying electricity from green electricity supplies; opting for the Fair Trade brands of coffee, tea, chocolate and other goods at the supermarket; and making a greater effort to buy wood and paper products from companies that ensure they have been made from renewable sources – that might cost a little more, but would make a huge difference. And identifying these goods is not difficult. Wind-powered electricity is available from npower. In the UK most supermarkets stock at least 70 Fair Trade products, and the Fair Trade kite mark guarantees that global corporations have not exploited poor farmers, nor kept farmworkers in near-slave conditions in the production of these goods. The Forest Stewardship Council mark ensures that wood and paper products come from renewable forests.

A fundamental discipline of Lent is almsgiving. First, this needs to be about money. We live in a materialistic culture, and what we do with our money is one of the surest indicators of where our priorities lie. Therefore, it is always important to give a sensible and realistic proportion of our income to support the work of the church and other charities that help alleviate suffering and its causes in the world. But Lent is a time when we can both review what we usually give, and give a little extra. As well as this, are there other ways in which we can expand our understanding of what it means to give? Why not look through the above list and decide what things you could and should be doing. These are simple disciplines we can easily build into a daily routine. Instead of just giving money to a good cause (though please don't stop doing this!) give something back to the planet as well. In so doing you will quench Christ's thirst.

And if you just want to do one small thing that can make a big difference, then take part in UNICEF's Jar of Grace Appeal. All you need to do is get a special leaflet from UNICEF. In the UK they are available from *The Jar of Grace Appeal*, UNICEF, Freepost, Chelmsford, CM2 8BR. With this comes a sticker you put on an empty jar, then at each mealtime you put a few coins (or notes!) into the jar. This campaign has run for a long while, but the current emphasis is on helping provide clean water for children around the world. UNICEF wants to raise money for oral rehydration sachets. They cost only seven pence each, but eight thousand children die daily from drinking dirty water. By ensuring this simple treatment is widely available, we could make a massive difference. At the end of the appeal – which could be done during Lent – the money from each jar is collected and sent to UNICEF.

Slaking a thirst closer to home

There are other ways we encounter the thirsty Christ. Giving money, and even making the lifestyle changes I have mentioned, are the easiest options. They make us feel good, and, as I have mentioned, some of them still save us money (though what we do with the money saved would be another good question to ask). But what about the need and poverty on our own doorstep, which we face each day, and so easily pass by? Here too we are challenged to give generously, for it is Christ who is thirsting in the homeless poor who haunt our cities, in the dispossessed and forgotten youth, in the drug dependent, the asylum seeker, the refugee. But perhaps this is the sternest challenge of all: dealing with a real person asking for money on the streets is much harder than putting a few pounds in an envelope, or instructing the bank to debit our account each month. And even as I write these sentences I am painfully aware that I prefer avoiding these situations and rarely feel I have dealt with them adequately.

I don't usually give money to people who beg on the streets. Sometimes I offer to buy them food or drink (though often this means they turn away from me). I then appease my conscience with the self-righteous satisfaction that they probably only wanted the money for drugs anyway. And probably they did, but this doesn't change the fact that this person is still my neighbour in Christ: the person in whom I can encounter Christ today.

However, there was an incident about a year ago when someone in the street stopped me and asked for money. And I gave my usual line, which was that I would buy them some food if that was what they wanted, but I could not give them money. They said food would be great. There was a McDonald's opposite (not my favourite eating-place) and I bought him some food there; we sat outside and chatted while he ate. It was good to talk to him, and good to listen to his story. And although when I left him I had not done much to improve his situation, neither did I feel that I had simply ignored or avoided him.

When writing this book I showed this chapter to someone who helpfully suggested that I go away and try making a more proper response to a beggar. 'Really and truly believe this is Christ standing in front of you, and see what happens – and then come back and write the paragraph again' is what they suggested. But I haven't done that. I have allowed myself to be busy. I have constructed plausible excuses.

But this is what we should be doing: treating each person we meet with respect and dignity as if they were Christ. I know this is the challenge I must face. Only last Sunday, as a big service was about to begin in Peterborough Cathedral, a man came to the sacristy door asking for money for a train fare. All of us were vested, the choir was in place, the service was due to begin. 'That's all we need now,' someone commented, 'a beggar!' But I was thinking, perhaps Christ had arrived at the service and we didn't give him any money, or even talk to him.

I think I need to learn how to offer myself in these situations: to learn how to listen and to explain why I am not giving any money if that is the decision I am taking. Usually, at the cathedral we offer food, and often this will be the most appropriate and practical thing to do. But let us at least ensure that we offer ourselves inasmuch as we treat those who come to us, and those we pass on the street, as brothers and sisters.

We need to find ways to engage with people as the beloved of God. In this way we keep the face of Christ before us in the faces of all whom we meet. We might even dare to hope that Christ is glimpsed in us. Moreover, we find that Christ is revealed in the exchange that takes place. There is a mutual enrichment that comes from a genuine engagement. I also believe that this engagement, however inadequate it feels, will motivate us to a greater involvement with groups who work to care for the homeless, or asylum seekers, or drug users, or whatever issue we face in our neighbourhood. And if you don't know about these groups, then walk the first mile of love and find out, and maybe focus your giving towards such a group. And if there are no groups in your neighbourhood, walk the second mile of love, make yourself vulnerable to the needs of others, and take a hand in organizing something. Every charitable organization that exists began because somebody cared enough to get something started (just one person made a difference). Often the church has been the catalyst for such endeavour, but it really doesn't matter who begins the work; it is a participation in God's purposes. Every church and every individual should ask themselves, 'How is my life, or the life of my church, a blessing to my community? How do we embody the tenacious love of God in the situations and lives we mix with each day?'

This, in turn, leads to deep changes of attitude within us. By being more involved in the care of our community, the way we feel about other people shifts. We no longer see people as problems that need solving, but as people who need loving.

Let me finish this section with one small story about changes in attitude, which, had I not written it down, only God and I would have known about. I believe it shows the way love can shape our inner motivations and have a profound influence on the way we live, the way we deal with others, and, ultimately, the way the whole world is shaped.

For the best part of five years I worked for an organization called Springboard, an initiative of the Archbishops of Canterbury and York for evangelism. This was, in the main, a travelling ministry, teaching, leading missions and running conferences around the country. Often I would stay at Retreat Houses where it is the custom that when you leave you make the bed for whoever will be using your room the next night. Clean bed linen is usually piled outside your door on the night before departure: you make up the new bed before breakfast and deposit the dirty sheets in laundry baskets at the end of each corridor. Over the years I don't know how many times I made a bed, and for the first few years I would moan and complain about having to under- take this chore. I would also enjoy cracking jokes at break- fast about how bad I was at making beds, and how sorry I felt for whoever got mine. But really this was an appalling attitude. For a start, making a bed is not that difficult a thing to do. Also, and more critically, I had lost touch with the fact that it was Christ who was sleeping in my bed that night. Now in some ways it may seem unbearably pious, or plain embarrassing, to say that I resolved to make the bed as carefully and as lovingly as I possibly could, but actually this relatively small change in attitude not only meant the bed got made better and the person who slept there enjoyed (I hope) a more comfortable night, but I also felt much happier. Now the job that had seemed such a tire- some bore, was one I actually enjoyed. Even in this small act of giving I received much.

A Final Thought

Jesus says in the Beatitudes, 'Blessed are those who hunger and thirst for righteousness, for they will be filled' (Matthew 5:6). As with all the Beatitudes, Jesus first of all describes himself. He is the one who hungers and thirsts to put things right, which is what happens on the cross – Jesus is putting the world right with God. Now as we look at him dying on the cross we realize we must do the same ourselves: we must hunger and thirst for things to be put right. And even if we do not see the completion of God's agenda for the world, his grace and peace will fill us, simply because we participated in Christ's thirsting love. 'Blessed are the merciful, for they will receive mercy' (Matthew 5:7).

For Discussion

Reflecting on God's Word

1 Read aloud Matthew 25:31–46 (or if you wish
  a shortened version, just up to v. 40).

2 Spend some time in silence.

3 Invite people to speak aloud into the silence a
  word or phrase that strikes them from the passage.

4 In pairs or small groups share with each other
  the words and phrases that have been spoken
  and how they relate to everyone's experience of
  encountering the thirsty Christ in the thirsting
  of the world.

Deepening our understanding of Lent

1 How are we using God's gifts to us in service to the 'least of these' – gifts of time, money, ability and so on?

2 How have we experienced the gospel taking us to places where we have become hungry or thirsty or in need of any kind? What were the circumstances? How did this feel?

3 What does it mean for us and for our church 'to hunger and thirst after righteousness'?

4 How can we expand our understanding of 'giving' so that it encompasses more than just money, but a giving of our whole lives in the service of the gospel? And if you need to keep the discussion practical (it is all too easy just to discuss this in theory), look again at the list of things to do on *p. 160*, and decide which of these you can take on.

For Reflection

Love is the power that transforms, because it invites our free co-operation with the process of transformation. Meekness is a trusting openness to God's purposes in our lives. Hungering and thirsting for righteousness is the expression of desire for the God who has met us in love, through Christ and by the Spirit. It expressed the response of love in desiring to join in with the purposes and concerns of the One who is loved.

This transformation takes place in a whole series of ways. *Our view of ourselves* is transformed because we discover we are loved by the God who made all that is and has created us to reflect something of his likeness in the world around. *Our view of the creation* is transformed: for we see it as made by God and made to fulfil his loving purposes. *Our view of others* is transformed: for we see God's image reflected in all other human beings. Moreover we also see other people as those through whom God speaks to and cares for us – giving love and affirmation and calling out our love and affirmation of others made in God's image. This profound shift in how we see God, others, ourselves and the world around us is called conversion.[8]

I was a revolutionary when I was young and all my prayer to God was 'Lord, give me the energy to change the world'.

As I approached middle age and realized that half my life was gone without my changing a single soul, I changed my prayer to 'Lord, give me the grace to change all those who come into contact with me. Just my family and friends, and I shall be satisfied.'

Now that I am old man and my days are numbered, my one prayer is 'Lord give me the grace to change myself'. If I had prayed for this right from the start I should not have wasted my life.[9]

For Prayer

O Lord, our hearts are heavy with the sufferings
of the ages, with the crusades and the holocausts
of a thousand thousand years.
The blood of the victims is still warm,
the cries of anguish still fill the night.
To you we lift our outspread hands.
We thirst for you in a thirsty land.

O Lord, who loves us as a father, who cares for us
as a mother, who came to share our life as a brother,
we confess before you our failure to love
as your children,
brothers and sisters bound together in love.
To you we lift our outspread hands.
We thirst for you in a thirsty land.

We have squandered the gift of life.
The good life of some is built on the pain of many;
the pleasure of a few on the agony of millions.
To you we lift our outspread hands.
We thirst for you in a thirsty land.

We worship death in our quest to possess
ever more things; we worship death
in our hankering after our own security,
our own survival, our own peace,
as if life were divisible, as if love were divisible,
as if Christ had not died for us all.
To you we lift our outspread hands.
We thirst for you in a thirsty land.

O Lord, forgive our life-denying pursuit of life,
and teach us anew what it means to be your children.
To you we lift our outspread hands.
We thirst for you in a thirsty land.[10]

CHAPTER 6

Living Water

On the last day of the festival, the great day, while Jesus was standing there, he cried out, 'Let anyone who is thirsty come to me, and let the one who believes in me drink. As the scripture has said, "Out of the believer's heart shall flow rivers of living water."'

JOHN 7:37–38

The death of Christ brings with it a terrible barrenness. As the few followers of Jesus who are at the cross traipse away they must experience a gnawing emptiness within, like a waterless, weary land. All their hopes have been nailed to the cross with Jesus, and now these hopes are gone. Jesus' body is taken down from the cross and laid in a tomb.

It must also have seemed as if Jesus himself had lost hope at the end. Standing there, watching him die, his friends would have admired his stoicism, they would have marvelled at his resilience and graciousness. But in the end that was all it was. Handed over to death, his crying out in thirst echoes the terrible words Mark recounts: 'My God, my God, why have you forsaken me' (Mark 15:34).

In the pattern of the church year Holy Saturday, the day between Good Friday and Easter Sunday, is a day of barren emptiness. It is the one day of the year when the Eucharist is not offered. In many churches all the ornaments and decorations are stripped away. There is no water in the font. All is lost and broken. The church beholds its Christ, and it beholds a lifeless corpse.

But in John's Gospel it is at this point, the precise point of death, where all seems lost, that the victory of the cross germinates. Indeed, Jesus had prepared his followers with these words: 'The hour has come for the Son of Man to be glorified. Very truly, I tell you, unless a grain of wheat falls into the earth and dies, it remains just a single grain; but if it dies, it bears much fruit' (John 12:23–24).

It seems as if faith and hope have been extinguished. Love appears to be beaten and buried. Yet it is the dead Christ who is the source of hope. Hence, we are led to the deepest mystery of all, the one we explore in this final chapter: Jesus, whom we see thirsting on the cross, is the source of living water. He is the one who will cleanse and revive us, the one who slakes our thirst.

Blood and water

After Jesus dies on the cross John records a strange and beautiful incident. The Jewish leaders do not want the crucified bodies left on the cross during the Sabbath, as it is against the law that criminals should remain on the cross after sunset (Deuteronomy 21:23). It is especially urgent on this day, since the following day is not only the Sabbath, but, according to John's scheme, the great feast of the Passover. The Roman custom, however, was to leave the corpse on the cross to act as a deterrent to others. Permission was needed to have the bodies removed, and, anyway, they might not yet be dead. So a request goes to Pilate that the legs of the crucified men be broken and the bodies be taken away (John 19:31–32).

Breaking the legs of men already in such torment seems, at first sight, a last unnecessary torture. However, it is an act of mercy designed to hasten death. By breaking the legs of the crucified, the dreadful cycle of shifting weight from nailed feet to suspended wrists is finally broken, and death comes swiftly. The soldiers knew what they were doing. This would finish off the gruesome job quickly, and deliver the dying men from what could sometimes be a very slow death.

First, they break the legs of the two criminals hanging alongside Jesus, but when they come to him they discover he is already dead (John 19:32–33). They are probably surprised at this. Hard though it is for us to imagine, six hours is a short time for a crucifixion. But, just to make sure, one of the soldiers pierces Jesus' side with a spear. And here is one of the most mysterious verses in the New Testament: 'at once', says John, 'blood and water came out' (John 19:34). John clearly attaches great importance to this event. It is from the dead body of the Saviour that the signs of new life flow.

Some years ago I remember seeing a documentary about the peace movement in the United States at the time of the Vietnam War. During the hot summer of 1968 – often referred to as the summer of love – there was a huge peace rally outside the Pentagon. Thousands of young people gathered to demonstrate against the war that was going so badly for the US, costing many lives and causing many problems. For the most part it was a peaceful occasion. But late in the afternoon, wanting to disperse the crowds, the military leaders inside the Pentagon sent out troops to break up the demonstration. The incident I now describe has become one of the most famous pieces of newsreel footage, summing up the spirit of the peace movement and how it tried to turn our world around. As the soldiers march in a straight line into the crowds, their rifles held out in front of them, cajoling them into returning home, a young man steps forward. He is holding a bunch of flowers. As the soldiers approach him he carefully places a flower in the barrel of one of the guns. It is a wonderful moment. Here are two young men facing each other, one armed with a rifle, the other with a flower. But the man with the gun is utterly powerless against the man with the flower. For when the flower is placed in the barrel of the gun, its menace is taken away. It is turned around. It has become a vase.

In the same way many people have wondered how it is that an instrument of such cruelty and torture – the cross – could come to be the primary symbol of a faith whose central tenets (despite the many failings of the church) are unity and peace. This may be the reason why it took so long for the cross to become the prime devotional symbol of the Christian faith. In fact, for the first few centuries of Christian history the cross was not the main symbol: it was the fish – a secret sign by which Christians recognized each other during persecution.[1] At first the memory – indeed the ongoing reality of crucifixion – was just too close for it to be used in any other way than the most obvious. Only after Constantine the Great, the first Christian emperor, abolished crucifixion in AD 337 did memories of this horrible form of death begin to fade and the cross begin to replace the fish as the pre-eminent Christian symbol.

From one perspective the cross is still an appalling symbol, similar in our own culture to a gas chamber or, more recently, the image of a plane hitting a tall building. You would not even think of casting such an image in silver and wearing it around your neck. All that is decent recoils from the horror of such a thought. Yet, to wear a cross around your neck, or put one up on a wall, is, on one level, just the same.

But the reason we now wear crosses and the reason why the cross became the pre-eminent symbol of the Christian faith was because its primary usage as an instrument of death was transformed. The resurrection of Jesus did not take away the horror, but it did change the way we interpret it. As the words of an ancient Christian hymn proclaim:

> The wood of the cross has become the tree of life
> Where life was lost, there life has been restored.

The triumph of the cross is victory over death, so Paul is able to cry out:

> Death has been swallowed up in victory.
> Where, O death, is your victory?
> Where, O death, is your sting? (1 Corinthians 15:54–55)

Through the resurrection of Jesus we have received a new perspective, a new way of seeing the whole of life, and therefore a new way of seeing death, however painful. The cross now symbolizes victory. It is the sign that tenacious love has defeated the powers of sin and death. It still reminds us of the horror and the pain, but now we see, even in this, the amazing transparency of God's complete participation in our life; it is the place where the self-emptying love of God is most complete. The cross is a meeting point between life and death, between despair and hope. It is a gateway into heaven, one that passes through the way of suffering and death.

To emphasize the reality and the mystery of the cross, some crosses and crucifixes are depicted with flowers growing from the places where Christ was nailed to the tree. The symbol of death is turned into a symbol of life: by his wounds we are healed. The cross contains both realities, God's complete sharing in humanity and God's complete victory over death. In this way we see that the triumph of the cross is the triumph of love.

In the book of the prophet Hosea is a strange little verse, which foreshadows this great Christian theme. The prophet says that God will draw his people into the wilderness and that he will 'make the Valley of Achor a door of hope' (Hosea 2:15).

The word 'achor' means 'bad luck' or 'despair'. Hosea is referring to a shameful episode in Israel's history where one person's disobedience to God led to military defeat. Great punishment was meted out to this person, and the place where he and his family were stoned to death and his possessions burned was called the Valley of Achor. We can read the gruesome story in Joshua 7:1–26.

But the astonishing thing the prophet is saying is that this place, the place of disobedience and despair, the place of shame and punishment, is also the place that will become the gateway to hope. It is a remarkable redefining of how God will deal with disobedience and failure. It points us forwards to the cross, the place where we see the worst of sin, but also the place where love is triumphant. On the cross sin, hurt and failure are dealt with. On the cross death is faced. The cross itself is the door of hope. The broken heart of Jesus is the gateway to life. Therefore, according to John's account, the one who thirsts is also the one from whom the living waters flow.

The prophet Isaiah also uses the dramatic imagery of water welling up in the desert to describe the renewal of the world, which will accompany God's judgement:

> The wilderness and the dry land shall be glad,
> the desert shall rejoice and blossom;
> like the crocus it shall blossom abundantly,
> and rejoice with joy and singing. (Isaiah 35:1–2a)

An abundance of water will increase the fertility of the land: God's kingdom will be established.

> Then the eyes of the blind shall be opened,
> and the ears of the deaf unstopped;
> then the lame shall leap like a deer,
> and the tongue of the speechless sing for joy.
> For waters shall break forth in the wilderness,
> and streams in the desert;
> the burning sand shall become a pool,
> and the thirsty ground springs of water . . .
> (Isaiah 35:5–7; see also Isaiah 41:17–20)

There is also here a reference back to the book of Exodus. After their deliverance at the Red Sea the people of Israel begin their great journey through the wilderness. Camping at Rephidim they find they have no water to drink. They quarrel among themselves and ask Moses to get them water. Why has Moses brought them out into the desert, only for them to die of thirst? Moses cries out to the Lord on behalf of the people and is told to go to the rock at Horeb. He strikes the rock, just as God instructs him, and water flows out for the people to drink (Exodus 17:1–7).

All this we also see happening on the cross. Here the waters of refreshment are flowing. This is the place of healing. This is the place where burdens can be laid down. It is the sign of God's rule on earth. The parched wilderness of the cross is now a flowing stream, the burning sand of Christ's thirst a spring of water. The dead wood of the cross has become the tree of life. The desert is coming into blossom. From the scars of passion flowers are growing. All this is captured in this moment of revelation. The soldiers pierce Christ's side – they reassure themselves he is dead – and from his side flows out blood and water. It is the first indication that the cross is not just another execution, not just another entry in the immense catalogue of human suffering, but is the axis of human history, the place where suffering and death are turned around.

This incident also points us towards the beginnings of the church. The church of Jesus Christ will be the people formed by the new covenant, and the two sacramental signs by which followers in the way of Christ will be incorporated and sustained in this new covenant are flowing from the broken heart of Jesus. The blood that flows from Christ's side reminds us again that he is the true Passover lamb. It is also a sign of the 'blood' we will share in the love feast of the Eucharist until that day when we will be with Christ in glory. As at the first Passover the blood of the lamb was painted on the doors so that the angel of death would pass by, now the blood of the true Lamb is shed that we might be saved from death. The water that flows from Christ's side reminds us of his words of promise that water will flow from the hearts of believers. It is also the sign of baptism, cleansing, redeeming and refreshing all those who die with Christ in order to share his risen life.

In John's Gospel the first sign (John doesn't call them miracles) is the changing of water into wine at the wedding at Cana (John 2:1–12). The abundance of wine produced is staggering. Six stone jars, each containing around 136 litres (30 gallons), are filled to the brim with water. When the chief steward tastes the water he discovers it to be the finest vintage. Although there were probably many other needs in the room, which most of us would deem a higher priority than producing this much wine for an already inebriated gathering of party-goers, Jesus is not now concerned with meeting needs – he is revealing the character of God. This is a sign not only of re-creation, taking and transforming the stuff of this world; it is a sign of profligate and extravagant love. This is what God is like, Jesus is saying.

In the following chapter a Pharisee, Nicodemus, visits Jesus in the night to discuss with him the meaning of his signs. Jesus tells him that no one, unless they be born again, can understand them. 'How can anyone be born after having grown old?' Nicodemus rather scornfully responds. 'Can one enter a second time into the mother's womb and be born?' Jesus replies, 'Very truly, I tell you, no one can enter the kingdom of God without being born of water and the spirit' (John 3:4–5). In the context of this passage Jesus may be referring to the baptism of repentance given by John the Baptist. But we cannot read this passage, and surely this is John's intention, without thinking of the Holy Spirit, and the waters of Christian baptism, and the dying and rising with Christ that they signify, and the living water of the Holy Spirit that is received.

Whoever believes in me will never be thirsty

In the fourth chapter of John's Gospel is an encounter between Jesus and a Samaritan woman at Jacob's well near the Samaritan city of Sychar (John 4:5–26). It is another story that begins with the words 'I thirst'.

It is noon, the hottest part of the day, and Jesus sits by the well. He is thirsty. The disciples have gone into the city to get some food and he probably has no means of drawing the water for himself.

A Samaritan woman comes to the well to draw water and Jesus asks her to give him a drink (John 4:7). This in itself is quite an astonishing thing to happen, and we see that the woman recognizes this by her slightly scornful reply 'How is it that you, a Jew, ask a drink of me, a woman of Samaria?' (John 4:9).

Jews and Samaritans, especially Jewish men and Samaritan women, were not supposed to mix. It was the Jewish

custom of the day that a man should not even salute a
woman in a public place, not even his own wife! William
Temple, in his wonderful commentary on St John's Gospel,
reminds his readers of the contempt in which women were
held. During the prayers of thanksgiving recited daily in the
synagogue the men would say, 'Blessed art thou, O Lord . . .
who hast not made me a woman.' And the women would
reply from the gallery, or another separate place, 'Blessed
art thou, O Lord, who hast fashioned me according to thy
will.' He adds, amusingly, 'if we now feel that the women
had the best of the exchange, that is a Christian and not an
ancient Jewish sentiment'.[2] Though, we might add, some
parts of the Christian church still have some catching up
to do in this regard.

But Jesus is able to ignore and transcend the prejudices
of his day. Not for the first time we see his remarkable attitude to women, giving them the full human dignity so often
denied them.

The enmity between Jews and Samaritans also raises
issues of race and religion. It is hard for us, reading the Bible
today, to understand the significance and implications of
the difference between these two religious groups. The
Samaritans shared an Israelite heritage, but since the time
of Babylonian exile their history had taken a different route,
and from the fourth century BC they had set up a temple at
Mount Gerizim in Samaria that was, to all intents and purposes, a rival to the temple in Jerusalem. We have already
discussed the huge significance of the temple to the Jewish
faith of Jesus' day, so it is not difficult to imagine the indignation and anger caused by the existence of this upstart,
alternative temple. This often boiled over into disorder. The
Roman historian Josephus mentions the violence that
occurred when Jews and Samaritans trespassed on to one

another's territory. Jews and Samaritans were enemies and there was great hatred between them. For a Jew a Samaritan was not just someone to avoid as unclean like a Gentile, a Samaritan was a heretic, an outcast, a half-breed and a rival.

In our day there are, sadly, other similar religious rivalries that continue to obscure our common humanity, and so often erupt into violence. The mistrust and hatred that existed between Jews and Samaritans is not so different from the situation in Northern Ireland between some Roman Catholics and some Protestants, or in the Holy Land between Jews ands Muslims, or in the Balkans between different Christian groups, or in the tribal conflicts that still disrupt many African states.

Hence, it is remarkable that Jesus makes the hero of his most famous story a Samaritan (see Luke 10:25–37). This story of a Jewish traveller falling among thieves, being ignored by the respectable and being cared for by a Samaritan, is so familiar to us that we do not think it has much to teach us beyond the fact that we should be generous to those in need. After all, the word 'Samaritan' in English usage has come to mean a good, kind person. (The organization that cares for those suicidal with despair is called the Samaritans.) But those hearing the story for the first time, all of them imagining themselves to be good Jews, would not have heard the story in this way. And they certainly would not have expected the hero of the story to be a good Samaritan.

They were expecting a story about a good Jew, someone like themselves – a story that heralded the triumph of the common man over the hypocrisy of lawyers and priests (people have always enjoyed a story that pokes fun at the establishment). But the sting in this tale does not allow you to associate yourself with the hero, because he turns out to be your sworn enemy, the very person you have spent your life dismissing and avoiding, the person you have demonized and considered less than human. Having laughed at the scribes and the Pharisees passing by on the other side, you find yourself left in the ditch. If you are not the Good Samaritan, then you must be the victim left by the side of the road.

You find to your amazement that your enemy is your neighbour. It is as if, in our own day, President George Bush were given the kiss of life by an al-Qaeda terrorist! Or an opponent of the ordination of women being helped by a woman priest. Now we begin to understand the words of this Samaritan woman. Why is a Jew, my enemy, asking me for water? Am I his neighbour? Should I give service to him?

But Jesus is, of course, untroubled, by these distinctions. Once again we see him happily crossing the boundaries that religion and politics and tradition love to erect. He is happy to receive water from her. But she is uncomfortable about offering it to him. He answers her, 'If you knew the gift of God, and who it is that is saying to you, "Give me a drink", you would have asked him, and he would have given you living water' (John 4:10).

At this point she misunderstands him. The phrase *living* water could just as likely mean *running* water. Is this not running water in the well? What is he on about? And anyway, she says to him, where will you get that living water without a bucket! 'Are you greater than our ancestor Jacob, who gave us the well?' (John 4:12). And here she gets in another little dig at the Jews – Jacob is our ancestor as well, she is saying.

Now we come to the crux of the story. There is a difference between the water that can be drawn from the well and the water Jesus is offering. 'Everyone who drinks of this water will be thirsty again', says Jesus, 'but those who drink of the water that I will give them will never be thirsty. The water that I will give will become in them a spring of water gushing up to eternal life' (John 4:13–14). William Temple puts it like this: 'The water in Jacob's well quenches thirst for the time; this other living water quenches for ever the thirst which it assuages, and is indeed an inward spring, bubbling up into eternal life.'[3]

At the wedding feast at Cana, Jesus turns the water into wine. Now he promises an inward spring, an elixir of life eternal, a source of refreshment, but also a flowing stream to bring life to others. The water Jesus is speaking of is the Holy Spirit. This could only be given when Jesus was glorified, and for John the glory of Christ is the cross. Here he is lifted up, and here he draws all people to himself.

But, unsurprisingly, the woman standing at the well with Jesus is not able to understand the implications of what he is saying. However, the encounter still has great meaning for her. For a start he treats her like a human being. And she certainly understands enough to say to him, 'Sir, give me this water, so that I may never be thirsty or have to keep coming here to draw water' (John 4:15).

A peculiar exchange follows. Jesus does not refuse to give her the water, but instead asks her to bring her husband so as he can share the gift as well. Her reply is economic with the truth. She says she has no husband. Reading her thoughts Jesus rightly pronounces that she has had five husbands and the present one, although she probably lives with him, is not legally or morally her husband at all. Straightaway, shamed and impressed by his insightful reply, the woman turns the agenda of the conversation to the vexed question concerning the place of true worship.

Should worship be offered on Mount Gerizim or in Jerusalem? But Jesus does not rule on this issue. Instead, he again transcends the current divide and points towards a new reality. His words describe the new covenant established on the cross, the precise reordering of creation that the soldiers carrying out their sordid duty at the cross, piercing the Lord's heart, have no idea they are witnessing:

> Woman, believe me, the hour is coming when you will worship the Father neither on this mountain nor in Jerusalem. You worship what you do not know; we worship what we know, for salvation is from the Jews. But the hour is coming, and is now here, when the true worshippers will worship the Father in spirit and truth, for the Father seeks such as these to worship him. God is spirit, and those who worship him must worship in spirit and truth. (John 4:21–24)

Jesus affirms the particular vocation of the Jewish people within God's plan for salvation. Salvation proceeds from the Jews; but it is not confined to them. The God whom they know and worship is revealed in Christ as the universal Father.[4] Moreover, Jesus says that 'God is spirit' (John 4:24).

This is a tremendously significant thing to say about God. It is saying that God is more than a kind of indwelling principle inherent in all created things, that he is not merely the totality of all that is, nor only the one whose ways are revealed in history. God is spirit – he is alive and active, with energy and purpose, but free of the temporal and spatial limitations characteristic of matter. He is not tied down to any one place. And he must be worshipped in spirit and truth, a worship that goes beyond adherence to any code or law to a true unity of heart and will, without hypocrisy or self-deception and according to the real nature of God, free from idolatry.

But again, the poor Samaritan woman listening to Jesus can make no sense of his words. They may be beautiful to us, looking back from the perspective of the cross and resurrection, but for her they must have seemed like pie in the sky, something that will be made plain only when the Messiah comes. On that day, she says to Jesus, 'he will proclaim all things to us' (John 4:25).

What follows is startling. Jesus says to her, 'I am he, the one who is speaking to you' (John 4:26).

I am the Messiah, the one who will reveal the truth about God, says Jesus. Even more profound for us reading John's account, the words 'I am he' could just as readily be translated, 'I am,' another example of Jesus using the sacred title of God to describe himself. I am the one through whom you will offer true worship, for I am the one in whom access to God is made available, through whom community with God is made possible. As blood and water flow from Christ's wounded side we discover him to be the source of life and refreshment for all thirst.

At this point we remember other Bible passages about water gushing from God. The prophet Ezekiel, for example, speaks of water flowing from the temple (Ezekiel 47:12). Wherever the water goes there is life and health. This powerful image is picked up in the book of Revelation. Right at the end of the book John is shown 'the river of the water of life, bright as crystal, flowing from the throne of God and of the Lamb' (Revelation 22:1). Immediately, we notice again the juxtaposition of the Old Testament image of the water of life flowing from the temple and the New Testament image of water flowing from Jesus, the Lamb. He has become the place where true worship is offered, where access to God is available, and where the water of life is found. Thus almost the last words in the Bible are these – Jesus speaking to his church:

> And let everyone who is thirsty come.
> Let anyone who wishes take the water of life as a gift.
> (Revelation 22:17b)

In John's Gospel, Jesus' final words are 'It is finished' (John 19:30), and then he dies. But Jesus is not just acknowledging the end of his life; he is also saying his mission is complete. He has become the one who thirsts, the one from whom the waters will now flow – he has opened the way of salvation.

Implications for Today

During this book we have explored five spiritual disciplines connected traditionally with Lent: fasting and self-denial, reading the Bible, self-examination and repentance, prayer, and almsgiving. Through them we have explored aspects of Christ's thirst for us and our thirst for him. It hardly needs saying that these disciplines need to be part of our lives throughout the year. Yet it is all too easy to read a book like this, feel reasonably committed to what it suggests, but fail to do much about it. Or else to make some real effort in Lent, only to let it all slip away when Lent is over.

Lent is a time of preparation for Easter. Easter is the feast of new beginnings, of new possibilities, of horizons expanded. Therefore, let Easter be your beginning, and use the celebration of Easter to make a fresh commitment to your own following in the way of Christ. The implications we will explore in this chapter are therefore to do with evangelism: how to be a witness to Christ in daily life, and also a final exploration of the meaning of Easter and baptism, the start of Christian faith and also the surest sign of the glory that awaits us. We also note again the dynamics of love, love's persistence being the ground of love's triumph.

The ministry of evangelism

We start with the story of the woman at the well. This story has some interesting implications for personal evangelism – the way we witness to our faith and share it with others, both in the church and as individual Christians. First, we notice that Jesus begins by receiving. Not as a strategy to begin a conversation, but out of a genuine need: he is thirsty. Too often the church begins its evangelism from a position of imagined power, offering to others what we think they need, rather than making ourselves vulnerable to their needs and questions, putting ourselves in a position where our own needs and vulnerabilities are apparent. It is, if you like, another small example of God's self-emptying love. He could be all-sufficient but he chooses not to be. As with the incarnation itself, he makes himself dependent on us. He asks for our service. In this instance he makes himself dependent on the woman to quench his thirst. The reason God chooses this way is that his concern is to create community, not display power. Others have made the point well, that God does not make us saints, and then give us work to do. He calls us to his service, and in the process we become saints. Likewise, in the ministry of evangelism, belonging comes before believing. People are called into a relationship in which their questions and concerns are taken seriously, where they are able to give as well as to receive, and then, in the context of these loving relationships, faith begins to grow. In other words, as we hear the call to enjoy community with God, often expressed in simple ways and through simple actions, we become aware of our own need of God. We reach a point where, like the woman in the story, we say to God, 'Give me this gift.'

But this is not the end of the story of evangelism, though you would be forgiven for thinking so in much of the Anglican Church. The story of our coming to faith does not end with our acknowledging our need of God, nor with God's promise that he will indeed quench our innermost thirsting. The Great Commission at the end of Matthew's Gospel does not say, 'Go into all the world and make converts.' Neither does it say, 'Go and make churchgoers.' The call of the gospel is to make *disciples*, to recognize that we have a share in his apostolic life. If we respond to this call, the living water we are given will gush forth from us to others; we are not supposed to keep it for ourselves. Indeed, if we try to, it will dry up within us. Hence, the joyless aridity of so much church life. That which was intended to be shared with all has been kept by a few, and in the keeping has evaporated away. What we are left with is the grim spectacle of empty worship, honouring the outward forms, but bereft of the inner spirit. This is like jumping into the shower each day to wash, although the water supply has been cut off years before, and not even realizing we are still dry and unclean!

The Roman Catholic documents on evangelization are particularly strong on this point. In an amazing passage they say:

> The Christian community is never closed in on itself. The intimate life of this community – the life of listening to the Word and the Apostles' teaching, charity lived in a fraternal way, the sharing of bread – only acquires its full meaning when it becomes witness, when it evokes admiration and conversion, and when it becomes the preach-

ing and proclamation of the Good News. Thus it is that the whole Church receives the mission to evangelize, and the work of each individual member is important for the whole.[5]

In other words, until you are living and sharing this faith there is a real sense in which you have not yet fully received it. This is precisely the same point I was making earlier about love. It is only when love persists and goes the second mile that its true nature is revealed.

In the last two chapters we have looked at examples of how people have loved tenaciously, sharing the living water of the gospel, and how they have put faith into action by meeting the needs of multitudes of hungry and thirsty people in the world. Here is a dynamic of giving and receiving, where our own thirst is quenched and where we become a source of refreshment to others. So, in this story, no sooner has the woman said she wishes to receive the water Jesus offers than he says to her, 'With whom will you share it?' This is the authentic sign of Christian discipleship: sharing with others what we have received. It is what the disciples did at Emmaus, having recognized Jesus in the breaking of the bread. It is the energy behind the whole mission of the church.

We give from the overflow of what we have received. We are drawn to receive because we experience the graciousness, the vulnerability and the acceptance of Christ embodied in his church. We ask God to bless and forgive us and to pour his spirit into us. He wants nothing more, but as he gives he turns us around so that we in turn may give to others, embodying his tenacious love and allowing ourselves to be vulnerable to others. Because we have assurance from God that he loves and forgives us, we find we have no fear. Unlike in the world, where we tend to ration generosity and love in case there is not enough to go round and we ourselves go short, we discover that it is in giving that we receive. The more we allow God to turn us around and serve him in the world, the more we experience the abundance of his blessing in our lives. It is as if that stream that flows from God is gushing within and through us.

David Watson, the great English evangelist, apparently said that if you are walking around with a cup full of water, if people bump into you they are bound to get wet! This is surely the best evangelism, the truly Christlike way of communicating the gospel. Not persuading people to believe, nor frightening them into submission with tales of hell, but being so filled with Christ that as people encounter us so they encounter him.

Baptism

Of course, some of us will not have this exciting and energizing experience of God's love bursting into us and out of us. Some of us might never have it, and most of us will feel it only rarely. This does not mean it is untrue: our feelings are not at all the best indicator of spiritual reality. But perhaps we are feeling rather tired in our faith, and this feeling of a faith that has dried up is getting in the way of renewal and mission, and, far worse, may lead to cynicism, self-obsession and fear. What is needed is a conscious renewal of our faith, a determined decision to love God and others, even if we do not *feel* very loving. Easter is an occasion to make such a decision. Many churches now have an affirmation of baptismal promises as part of their Easter worship.

These are the questions asked in the new initiation services of the Church of England:

Do you reject the devil and all rebellion against God?

Do you renounce the deceit and corruption of evil?

Do you repent of the sins that separate us from God and neighbour?

Do you turn to Christ as Saviour?

Do you submit to Christ as Lord?

Do you come to Christ, the way, the truth and the life?[6]

The language is uncompromising and robust. But these provide an opportunity to make an act of will: a fresh response to God's love. First, we are called to turn away from evil, rebellion and sin and turn instead to Christ. We have already explored in previous chapters the important place repentance has in the Christian life. The impetus of these promises is to move beyond the sorrow of repentance to what it means to live as a baptized person each day. What does it mean each day to live with the reality of turning to Christ, submitting to his will, and discovering him to be the way, the truth and the life?

In this way we discover that baptism is not an isolated event – something that happened to us in the past and that we are now moving away from. Rather, it is a present reality, an identity that shapes us, a yardstick by which we measure our every thought, action and word. It is a call to be Christlike, transparent in our faith, so that Jesus' way, truth and life are manifest in us. This affects much more than our feelings, and will be evident in the decisions we take, in how our character is formed and in how we live.

If Lent is a time of preparation for Easter, then it is a time when we can consider what it means to live by the promises of our baptism. All the disciplines of Lent that we have been looking at in this book are about schooling us in the way of Christ's love so that we may live a Christlike life (even if we do not feel very Christlike!). Just as the cross and the resurrection only make sense in relation to each other, so the fast of Lent only acquires its full meaning when related to the feast of Easter, to which it looks forward and prepares. At Easter we celebrate the great victory of God's purposes for the world, the seal and vindication of Christ's tenacious loving, and the inundation of living water through the outpouring of the Spirit. It is through these living waters that we have been brought into community with God. We now resolve to live as channels of the same.

I recently preached at St Jude's Church in Peterborough on their patronal festival. Like many preachers before me I guess I began my sermon with words of apology, explaining that not much is known about St Jude. In fact, the only time he is recorded as saying anything is on the night before Jesus' death. But his question to Jesus is very interesting. Jude says to Jesus, 'Lord, how is it that you reveal yourself to us, and not to the world?' (John 14:22). This echoes the question many of us have asked of God: 'Why is it, God, that some people believe and others don't? Why is it that you don't make yourself known in that person's life, or in that situation?' Many of us are pained by the fact that those we love most do not share our faith. Many of us are bewildered by what seems to be God's lack of activity in the world. Why do you reveal yourself to us, but not to the world, we say with Jude, and wait for an answer.

We could read all that follows in the next couple of chapters of John's Gospel as Jesus' answer to this question. But let us look particularly at two things Jesus says in John's account. His immediate reply to Jude is this: 'Those who love me will keep my word, and my Father will love them, and we will come to them and make our home with them' (John 14:23). Jesus' answer is at first glance only further confirmation that God will be revealed to Jude. It is, however, a very strong affirmation. It is not just about being known, but about a complete indwelling, an abiding in love – we will come to them and make our home with them. Notice also the use of the plural: this is the Father and the Son who will make *their* home in the hearts of the beloved.

But then Jesus goes on, 'I have said these things to you while I am still with you. But the Advocate, the Holy Spirit, whom the Father will send in my name, will teach you everything, and remind you of all that I have said to you' (John 14:25–26).

This is further affirmation of God's presence, now promised in an even richer, more dynamic way: the outpouring of the Spirit. But there is also something enigmatic about these words; they have a cutting edge to them. 'The Holy Spirit will teach you everything,' says Jesus; that is, the Holy Spirit would remind them of what he had said. 'I am going to the Father' (John 14:28), Jesus continues, 'But if you abide in me and let me abide in you, you will bear much fruit . . . You will be my witnesses' (John 15:5,27[7]).

In other words, we could drastically paraphrase Jesus' reply like this: 'Yes, Jude, I do indeed intend to make myself known to the world. And this is how I propose to do it – through you!'

This is the astonishing end to the gospel story as we read it in the New Testament. The mission of God's love made known to us in Jesus Christ is entrusted into the hands of Jesus' followers. That ragtag, Keystone Cops, barmy-army band of disciples will become the vehicle through which God's grace will be dispensed throughout the world. Left to our own devices, reliant on our own strength, nothing much would happen. But affirmed by love, energized by grace, propelled by the Spirit, all things are possible. The story of the Christian church is really the story of persistent love flowing from the cross of Jesus through the hearts of men and women to a thirsty world.

Baptism is the means by which we enter this great story of God's love. In baptism we die with Christ, are drowned in the deep waters of death. In baptism we rise with Christ, are saved and refreshed – the living waters of the Holy Spirit are lavished upon us.

The best way to use Lent is to use it to get ready for Easter, to use it as a way of preparing for that moment when you can reaffirm your commitment to Christ and his way of tenacious love. When you stand in church on Easter day and renew your promises, say them with the same determined joy as if they were your last words before a firing squad. Be defiant against all the false promises of the world: 'I turn to Christ.'

Take this all of you and drink

Someone recently asked me when I felt closest to God. There are many answers I could have given: listening to music has always been an intensely spiritual experience for me, and as I mention in the acknowledgements at the end of this book I always write with music playing. During the writing of this book I have listened again and again to James Macmillan's beautiful piece of music *Seven Last Words from the Cross*. This music has helped me to imagine myself at the cross, to feel something of the passion and beauty of Christ's suffering.

I also feel close to God in the company of the people I love the most. I feel close to God when I am alone in the countryside, especially if it is somewhere wild and lonely. I love extremes of weather: driving rain, or snow, or intense heat. But on that occasion I did not mention any of these things. I came out with what may seem a rather churchy answer: straightaway I said that I felt closest to God when I baptize people into the community of the church and invite them to receive communion. These two acts that I perform on behalf of the church are part of the great privilege of my ministry as a priest. Even though I have done them many, many times they always move me.

I love that moment in the baptismal service when a tiny baby is entrusted into my hands, and holding it over the font I pour upon its forehead the living water. I love the moment of invitation in the Eucharist when I hold a broken piece of bread and bid the faithful to share in the supper of the Lord.

In both these ministries I find myself trembling with expectation at the immensity of the trust God has placed in me in letting me touch and administer these holy things. I know I am entrusted to do this not because of my worthiness or skill, but simply because of God's love for me. It is my share in the priesthood of Christ. I stand at the font, or I stand at the altar and I become most fully the person God made me to be. In the beautiful words of Thomas Merton, describing how he felt when celebrating the Eucharist, I feel 'washed in the light that is eternity and become one who is agelessly reborn'.[8] And often I find myself wanting to stop and hold these beautiful moments: that moment of baptism as the waters tumble and break, that moment of invitation as the broken bread is held aloft. It is these moments that are for me the purest moments of adoration, the times when I feel closest to God. These are the times I know him as the one who wipes away my tears, who whispers words of love and affirmation in my ear, who calms the fever in my brow, who slakes my thirst. This, for me, is true worship, a foretaste of what heaven will be, a beginning of eternal life in the clamour of the life that is here and now. Adoration, says William Temple, is 'the most selfless emotion of which our nature is capable and therefore the chief remedy for that self-centredness which is our original sin and the source of all actual sin'.[9] It is not that I lose myself in these moments of adoration and closeness to God; it is rather that, at last, I am found. I discover for a few moments the living reality of that which I talk about so much: I have become myself in communion with God.

As the living waters flow through my fingers to the head of God's beloved, as God's faithful people hold out their hands to receive the bread of the Eucharist, I feel the Holy Spirit flooding through me, cleansing me, anointing me, raising me, bringing me into the graceful embrace of God. I am taken up into the dance that is God's joyful union. I am set free to be myself. It is as if the water and blood that flowed from Christ's heart are nourishing me, filling me, replenishing me, creating me and flowing through me to the thirsty of the world. As the psalmist says:

> You anoint my head with oil;
> my cup overflows. (Psalm 23:5)

In which case, why don't we shout this from the rooftops? Why are we so tongue-tied and reluctant to tell people of the love of God? Why are the doors of our churches locked? Why are we so quick to cloak the transparent joy of our faith with the worn out, counterfeit clothing of the world?

We should be inviting all and sundry to the waters of baptism. We should love nothing more than to bring people to the Eucharist, the great love feast of the Christian church. We should faint with joy when the priest invites us to eat and drink, and to receive the body and blood of Jesus, his life given for us. We should be longing for Easter when we can renew our own promises to Christ.

There is this tension within us, and while it remains, the world carries on groaning in travail as we await our redemption. Jesus still hangs upon the cross: 'I am thirsty,' he cries.

A Final Thought

There is one last incident in the Gospels to refer to. In Mark's Gospel, just before Jesus enters Jerusalem, James and John ask him if they can sit on his right hand and his left in glory (Mark 10:37). Jesus replies, 'You do not know what you are asking. Are you able to drink the cup that I drink, or be baptized with the baptism that I am baptized with?' (Mark 10:38). God addresses the same question to us. Can we be baptized with the baptism of Christ? Can we drink the cup he sets before us? Are we willing to discover what it means to be a disciple of Jesus Christ? Are we able to share in Christ's suffering love? Here is the paradox of our faith: the one who refreshes is also the one who needs to be refreshed. The one who offers me the water of life is also the one who is dying of thirst. The one who thirsts is also the one in whom my thirst is quenched.

For Discussion

Reflecting on God's Word

1 Read aloud the final part of the passion narrative in John's Gospel from John 19:16–37.

2 Spend some time in silence.

3 Invite people to speak aloud into the silence a word or phrase that strikes them from the passage.

4 In pairs or small groups share with each other the words and phrases that have been spoken and how they shed fresh light on the passion of Jesus.

Deepening our understanding of Lent

1 What does the phrase 'I thirst' now mean to you?

2 How might the challenge to live and share your faith also enable you to receive it more fully?

3 Can you drink the cup the Father puts before you? Can you be baptized with the baptism Jesus offers? What does this challenge mean to you, and what difference is it going to make in your life?

4 Share with one another the moments when you feel closest to God.

For Reflection

Good Friday at the L'Arche community: day of the Cross, day of suffering, day of hope, day of abandonment, day of victory, day of mourning, day of joy, day of endings, day of beginnings.

During the liturgy . . . P're Thomas and P're Gilbert took the huge cross that hangs behind the altar from the wall and held it so that the whole community could come and kiss the dead body of Christ.

They all came, more than four hundred people – handicapped men and women and their helpers and friends. Everybody seemed to know very well what they were doing: expressing their love and gratitude for him who gave his life for them. As they were crowding around the cross and kissing the feet and the head of Jesus, I closed my eyes and could see his sacred body stretched out and crucified upon our planet earth. I saw the immense suffering of humanity during the centuries: people killing each other; people dying from starvation and epidemics; people driven from their homes; people sleeping on the streets of large cities; people clinging to each other in desperation; people flagellated, tortured, burned, and mutilated; people alone in locked flats, in prison dungeons, in labor camps; people craving a gentle word, a friendly letter, a consoling embrace, people – children, teenagers, adults, middle-aged and elderly – all crying out with an anguished voice: 'My God, my God, why have you forsaken us?'

Imagining the naked, lacerated body of Christ stretched out over our globe, I was filled with horror. But as I opened my eyes I saw Jacques, who bears the marks of suffering in his face, kiss the body with passion and tears in his eyes. I saw Ivan carried on Michael's back. I saw Edith coming in her wheelchair. As they came – walking or limping, seeing or blind, hearing or deaf – I saw the endless procession of humanity gathering around the sacred body of Jesus, covering it with their tears and their kisses, and slowly moving away from it comforted and consoled by such great love. There were sighs of relief; there were smiles breaking through tear-filled eyes; there were hands in hands and arms in arms. With my mind's eye I saw the huge crowds of isolated, agonizing individuals walking away from the cross together, bound by the love they had seen with their own eyes and touched with their own lips. The cross of horror became the cross of hope, the tortured body became the body that gives new life, the gaping wounds became the source of forgiveness, healing and reconciliation. P're Thomas and P're Gilbert were still holding the cross. The last people came, knelt, and kissed the body, and left. It was quiet, very quiet.

P're Gilbert then gave me a large chalice with the consecrated bread and pointed to the crowd standing around the altar.

I took the chalice and started to move among those whom I had seen coming to the cross, looked at their hungry eyes, and said, 'The body of Christ . . . the body of Christ . . . the body of Christ' countless times. The small community became all of humanity, and I knew that all I need to say my whole life long was 'Take and eat. This is the body of Christ.'[10]

I heard the voice of Jesus say,
'Come unto me and rest;
Lay down, thou weary one, lay down
Thy head upon my breast':
I came to Jesus as I was,
Weary, and worn, and sad;
I found in him a resting place,
And he has made me glad.

I heard the voice of Jesus say,
'Behold, I freely give
The living water, thirsty one;
Stoop down, and drink, and live':
I came to Jesus, and I drank
Of that life-giving stream;
My thirst was quenched, my soul revived,
And now I live in him.[11]

For Prayer

Almighty God, we thank you for our fellowship in the household of faith with all those who have been baptized in your name. Keep us faithful to our baptism, and so make us ready for that day when the whole creation shall be made perfect in your Son, our Saviour, Jesus Christ. Amen.[12]

The Story of the Cross

From the very beginning God has made human beings free, free to accept his love and his ways, but also free to reject them. The story of Adam and Eve is a story of God's purpose, and also a story of how God's purpose was rejected. These archetypal human figures express their freedom by rejecting God's ways and God's love. But God does not reject them. Neither does he ever abandon his beloved. He finds a way to show what total love, total obedience and true freedom actually look like. First, he does this through a people. He chooses the wandering Hebrew tribes and through them seeks to disclose his love and foster his way. Abraham is the father of this great people, and their story is one of struggle and delight. From slavery in Egypt they are led to liberty and prosperity. They are given a land of their own. They are given a law that shapes their life and channels their freedom. In a world of competing deities, it is revealed to them that there is only one God, and it is from this one God that the whole creation has its being. Ironically, this great message of God's unity of purpose actually sets them apart from other peoples. Yet they also know it will be through them that everyone will eventually come to know God's love. This is their great hope, their vocation.

There are times when this people again reject their God. There are times of astonishing insight when their prophecies and wisdom strike right to the heart of God, in ways they are not even themselves yet able to grasp or comprehend. They have their great heroes, like Moses and David, but they also have their villains. Sometimes, as is often the way, their greatest heroes are also their greatest sinners. And thus it is that their story resonates with the whole human story. But throughout the journey of their history they are never able to fulfil their vocation so completely that the light of God given to them can also shine for the whole world to see. Sin, the misuse of freedom, the false north of self-centredness and pride, again and again obscures the light of their calling and dulls their message. Their temple is destroyed and they are exiled. A pattern of acceptance and fresh beginning, followed by dereliction and failure, take hold. There seems no way that human beings on their own can remain free, and freely find communion with God.

But all the while this people hold on to their great hope that God will raise up for them a new king – an anointed one, a messiah – who will re-establish their kingdom, sweep away their enemies, and restore their fortunes, one through whom God will powerfully be at work.

And neither does God abandon his favour or lose sight of his goal. These are the people he loves, and through love of them God longs for communion with all. He will send a messiah, but it will not be as his people expect. God will communicate his love in the only way the world is able to receive it: by becoming part of the creation he has made, by speaking the language of the world, and by turning the expectations of the world upside down. The might God will demonstrate will be the mighty power of gentleness and love.

Thus the whole story and vocation of God's people comes to balance on the axis of a young woman's response to the request that she might be the one who will bear the Messiah of God, so that God himself can breathe the air of his creation and save it from itself. Her response must be free, such is the way of love. She could have said no. And at this great moment in the story of salvation we see the true courtesy of love. The God who made the heavens and the earth waits upon the response of his creation. Mary's yes to God is the turning point of human history, his birth among us the point at which our calendars change.

He is given the name Jesus, which means 'God saves'; and in his life he seeks to fulfil the vocation of Israel his people – to be faithful to God, to live a life of perfect obedience and love, and to become the Lamb of God who takes sin away. He is also called Emmanuel, which means 'God is with us', because the first message of his life, the means by which the divine communication will take place, is that God now dwells with his people, sharing completely in their life.

As this man grows up, because he is a real man like every other, he experiences the challenges, temptations and constraints all human beings know. He feels joy and sadness, exhilaration and pain. He is uncertain how he must live out his vocation. He is travelling a way no one has gone before. He must walk in a way that embodies the message of perfect love. He searches the Scriptures of his people for insight and understanding. He discovers there ia a way of servanthood and seeks to live it to the full.

All the while his communion with God gives him power and authority of a kind people have not witnessed before. He disturbs the religious leaders of his day. He becomes the focus of all sorts of misplaced hopes and anxious fears. He upsets the political equilibrium of his occupied land. The hope he finds in Scripture resonates with the experience of his life. He begins to see more clearly that his way must lead to suffering and death, and though still fearful, he embraces this as the way God intends. Handed over to suffering, silent before his accusers, he fulfils all that the Law requires, all that the Scriptures foretell: he becomes the suffering servant of God. Dying on the cross and in fulfilment of the Scriptures, which have shaped his vocation, he cries out, 'I thirst'.

His death is the sacrifice for sin, a perfect offering to God, a perfect demonstration of love, a perfect obedience to the will of God, a perfect expression of the freely offered choice to love. He could have followed a number of other routes. He chooses not to. He embraces the way of suffering love. 'By his wounds we are healed' was the ominous foretelling of the Hebrew prophet Isaiah, in words he himself could not have understood.

'It is finished,' the dying man cries out. Divinity is perfectly united with humanity. The God who emptied himself in love to become human has now plumbed the depths of human experience. The one who shared our birth also shares our death. Reconciliation with God is achieved. A change has taken place, but its implications are still hidden. Such is the way of love. For three days it lay dormant in the corpse of an executed man. But perfect love endures all things. It goes on. In the small hours of the night, on the third day after the crucifixion, God raises Jesus to life. He still bears the marks of suffering, and he will bear them for eternity as the final sign of God's passionate love for his creation. But tenacious love, God's love, cannot be defeated. And from his broken heart the living waters flow.

At first he is not recognized. Mary Magdalene, one of the women in the group, mistakes him for the gardener.

Two friends leaving Jerusalem for Emmaus are captivated by his words, as he opens up the Scriptures for them, but they do not know who it is who is walking with them. This also is the way of love. God will not do anything to jeopardize or take away our freedom to choose how we respond to what he has done for us in Christ. Not because he is testing us, nor playing tricks on us, nor making it hard for us, but because he loves us so much. He longs only for the free response of our love to the love he has lavished upon us in Christ. It is like being adopted into a new family, says the great apostle Paul; the offer of the Christian faith is not to be slaves of Christ, nor servants of Christ, nor even friends of Christ, but co-heirs to eternal life, blood brothers and sisters, with all the rights and benefits that go with family membership.

Through the cross a way is made from earth to heaven. 'I am going now to prepare a place for you' is one of the last things Jesus says to his friends. It is an astonishing claim, what the church calls the 'gospel': good news of eternal life, good news that sin and death have been defeated. We will still sin, and we will still die, but they no longer have the last word. They met their match in Christ. What did he do? Well, he just couldn't stop loving them. They did their worst, and he still loved them. And he extends that love to us. He can't make us love him, but he will wait forever in the hope that we might love in return. And even if we don't, even if no one does, it does not change what he has done; it does not stop him loving.

It is like a marriage, says St Paul, referring to the relationship between Christ and his people, the church. On the cross God pledges his troth to us. I will go on loving and cherishing you in sickness and in health. Now he waits for us to pledge our troth to him. He can't make us do this. If he could, it wouldn't be love. That is why he always comes among us in ways not immediately recognized. He is the stranger at our side, warming our hearts, the unseen voice calling our name. But wherever we glimpse the possibilities and capacities of human love, we are close to the heart of Christ and experience his love for us.

To walk the Christian way is to live as those who turn to Christ, who return his love. This way begins with the free response of the human spirit to the love of God. It is marked in the waters of baptism. It needs to be renewed every day. It cries out to be manifest in the lives we lead. Our vocation is to be the people of the cross: tenacious lovers, persistent in our generosity, resolute and obedient to building God's kingdom in the world.

What can love do? Well, all that love can do is go on loving. It has no choice. It either loves, or it stops being love. On the cross we see the perfect love of God revealed in painful detail: a tenacious, resolute and persistent love; a love that goes the second mile, that turns the other cheek, that will not coerce or give way – a love that triumphs.

When we read the story of Christ's passion, or look at a cross, or simply imagine what Jesus endured on that Friday afternoon long ago, we see the immense capacity of God to go on loving. We also see that all this was achieved for us. It was for our salvation that God thirsted so much. And now we must do the same. We place our hands in the living water, we trace the mark of the cross on our bodies, and we commit ourselves to God's cause in the world.

O come Holy Spirit, reveal your presence in me,
make my heart a dwelling place for God.
Disclose through me the mysteries of your love.
Use me for your purpose in the world.
Release in me the energy of grace.
Unfold in me the person of your Son.
I am thirsty Lord, give me a drink.
You are thirsty, Lord; it is not much, but let me give you
     what I can.
And all because in your cross heaven and earth are wedded
     together,
forever and forever. Amen.

The Rising

From the scars of passion flowers grow,
bearing fruit where life was lost and flawed.
In the desert healing waters flow,

valleys lifted, mountains now laid low,
where the heart was frozen it is thawed.
From the scars of passion flowers grow,

the mended tissue, stronger, starts to glow
like stars ablaze where pain had been ignored.
In the desert healing waters flow,

in the places where you feared to go,
release from all the bitterness you stored.
From the scars of passion flowers grow,

reconciling all you did not know,
making peace with all that was deplored.
In the desert healing waters flow,

reaping harvests that you did not sow;
where life was lost, there life has been restored.
From the scars of passion flowers grow,
in the desert healing waters flow.

Acknowledgements

Oscar-winning actors are prone to blurt out hearty thanks
to every person they have ever known. It is not always an
edifying spectacle and I fear I am in danger of doing the
same thing here. Yet every book, though usually written by
one person, is always the work of many. As I have written
this I have been very conscious of the influence of others
who have shaped and directed my understanding of the
Christian faith. I cannot list them all, but I am heartily
thankful for their wisdom. Behind this book lie the ser-
mons, books, articles, encouragement, exhortations and,
most of all, loving examples, of many good Christian men
and women.

This book is also the tale of two archbishops. Archbishop
George Carey wrote to me several years ago to ask if I would
be interested in writing a future Archbishop's Lent book. I
was excited and daunted by the prospect, not least by the
free hand I was given as to what the book should be about.
In the past the books I have written have tended to be com-
missions, written on specific subjects requested by the publishers. This was the first time I could actually *choose* what
to write about.

I had been brooding upon Jesus' words from the cross
'I thirst' for some time and in my initial letter to the publishers

I described the idea for the book as 'an extended meditation on these words of Christ from the cross'. The idea seemed worth pursuing, but no sooner had I begun writing than I heard the news of Archbishop George's retirement. I was then told that a new archbishop (whoever that was going to be) would have to be consulted about who would write what would be his first Lent book. This uncertainty was hardly the best incentive to keep writing, but I felt I had the book within me, so kept on, hoping that the idea would find favour with the new archbishop once he was chosen.

Like many in the church I greeted the appointment of Rowan Williams with great excitement. I was also delighted (and somewhat relieved!) to hear that he was happy for me to continue with the book. I hope this book repays a little of the trust these two godly men have had in me.

I have also hugely enjoyed writing it. Writing has always been a great passion of mine, and I find when I write I get completely lost in and consumed by what I am doing. The book poured out of me, and I found the experience of writing it a real experience of the presence of God. In fact, for me, the creative act of writing is a prayer. And I am very conscious of the directing and inspiring of the Holy Spirit as I write. It also comes from my heart. Through this book I have found opportunity to give voice to the things that matter to me most about the Christian faith. My hope and prayer is that it may now be an inspiration and a resource for others.

As I have written, I have nearly always had music playing. Many times I have listened to James MacMillan's *Seven Last Words from the Cross*. It is a desperately beautiful piece of music. His setting of the words 'I thirst' has the two words themselves sung over and over again, drawn out in a static monotone. Words from the Good Friday Reproaches are whispered urgently by the chorus, while crescendos of strings quiver like a cloud of approaching locusts, and then dissolve. The heat and wretchedness of Christ's thirst are hauntingly evoked.

I can't say how much this piece of music has shaped what I have written, but I have felt a great need to turn to it again and again to feel myself at the cross as I have tried to convey something of its beauty, its starkness and its truth; and I wanted to acknowledge this music's importance to me in the process of writing this book.

There are a few other individuals whom I wish to thank. My colleagues at Peterborough Cathedral have been very supportive as I have fitted in the writing of this book around my other commitments at the cathedral. Canon Bill Croft has read through several of the chapters and helpfully raised many issues. Claire Foster, advisor in science, medicine, technology and environmental issues, at the Public Affairs Unit in Church House, Westminster, gave me some challenging advice for Chapter 5. My personal assistant, Helena del Pino, has made a number of helpful suggestions as well as providing practical help in the completion of the final text. Amy Boucher Pye, Acquisition Editor at Zondervan, has also been very encouraging. A fine lunch when we first met in London got the project off to a good start. A steady flow of emails have kept me on course. Carolyn Armitage has edited the book. Although at the time of writing I have not met her, her detailed comments on the text and her many suggestions as to where the book's intentions can be clarified and distilled have been hugely beneficial. I am sure that the final flow of the book owes a great deal to her patient reading of the text and her considerate and insightful reflections. I look forward to meeting her in person to say thank you. In the meantime I hope these few words will indicate the debt of thanks I owe. Angela Scheff, Associate Editor at Zondervan, has also helped enormously with the final edit.

Finally, I wish to acknowledge and give thanks for the help, constant support, good-humoured resilience and cheerful encouragement of my wife, Rebecca, to whom I dedicate this book, and without whom I would not be able to do the things I do.

Stephen Cottrell
Holy Week 2003

Notes

Introduction

1 'An Order for the Beginning of Lent', in *Lent, Holy Week and Easter, Services and Prayers, Commended by the House of Bishops of the General Synod of the Church of England*, Church House Publishing / Cambridge University Press / SPCK, 1984, pp. 14–15.

2 N. T. Wright, *The Challenge of Jesus*, SPCK, 2000, p. 69.

3 Eric Milner-White, 'Lent', in his *My God, My Glory*, SPCK, 1954, p. 21.

4 Frank Colquhoun, *Contemporary Parish Prayers*, Hodder and Stoughton, 1975, p. 80.

Chapter 1. The God Who Shares

1 In this form found in *Celebrating Common Prayer*, Mowbray, 1992, pp. 219–20.

2 The Creed of St Athanasius, found in this form in *Patterns for Worship*, Church House Publishing, 1995, p. 59.

3 'Prayer of Commendation from Ministry at the Time of Death', in *Common Worship: Services and Prayers for the Church of England, Pastoral Services*, Church House Publishing, 2000, p. 229.

4 'An Order for the Beginning of Lent', in *Lent, Holy Week and Easter, Services and Prayers, Commended by the House of*

Bishops of the General Synod of the Church of England,
Church House Publishing / Cambridge University Press /
SPCK, 1984, p. 26.

5 Julian of Norwich, *Revelations of Divine Love*, trans. Clifton
Wolters, Penguin Books, 1966, pp. 88–90.

6 Gerard Manley Hopkins, selected and with an introduction
by W. H. Gardner, *Poems and Prose*, Penguin Books, 1953,
p. 67.

7 Thomas Traherne, *The SPCK Book of Christian Prayer*,
SPCK, 1995, p. 196.

Chapter 2. The Word That Shapes

1 Steven Croft, *The Lord Is Risen*, Emmaus Bible Resources,
National Society / Church House Publishing, 2001.

2 Ibid., p. 45.

3 Ibid.

4 These two observations, about the way Jesus and Philip
approach the task of communicating the gospel by meeting
people where they are and listening before they speak, are
of great significance for the ministry of evangelism today.
A longer discussion of the implications of this can be found
in S. Cottrell, S. Croft, J. Finney, F. Lawson and R. Warren,
Emmaus: The Way of Faith: Introduction, National Society /
Church House Publishing, 1996.

5 Croft, *Lord Is Risen*, p. 84.

6 'An Order for the Beginning of Lent', in *Lent, Holy Week
and Easter, Services and Prayers, Commended by the House of
Bishops of the General Synod of the Church of England*,
Church House Publishing / Cambridge University Press /
SPCK, 1984, p. 15.

7 My book *On This Rock*, Bible Reading Fellowship, 2003,
is written to help people begin reading the Bible regularly.

8 Henri Nouwen, *Seeds of Hope*, Darton, Longman and Todd, 1989, p. 70.

9 From Stephen Cottrell and Steven Croft, *Travelling Well: A Companion Guide to the Christian Faith*, Church House Publishing, 2000, p. 43.

10 Dick Williams, *The SPCK Book of Christian Prayer*, SPCK, 1995, p. 386.

Chapter 3. The Call to Be Thirsty

1 There are different accounts of the institution of the Eucharist at the Last Supper, but they all follow a pattern that is already liturgical, showing how the breaking of bread in this way had quickly become part of the life of the early church. See Matthew 26:26–29; Mark 14:22–25; Luke 22:14–22; 1 Corinthians 11:23–26. Indeed, in Paul's account, probably the earliest of the three, he begins by saying, 'For I received from the Lord what I also handed on to you . . .' (1 Corinthians 11:23 NRSV), clearly implying an existing tradition.

2 John's Gospel doesn't contain an account of the Last Supper. John has a different chronology for the events of Jesus' passion. As mentioned earlier, he makes the day of the crucifixion the day of Passover, timing the death of Jesus to the exact point that the Passover lambs were being slaughtered in the temple.

3 A difficult word to translate, it probably means 'oil press'. This places the action near the Mount of Olives, the location Luke names.

4 Fiona MacCarthy, *Stanley Spencer: An English Vision*, Yale University Press, 1997, p. 104.

5 People who know my work with Springboard, the Archbishop's initiative for evangelism, will have heard me speak about these paintings, which always evoke a powerful

reaction: not least, people want to know where they can get copies! Most books on Spencer contain reproductions.

6 N. T. Wright, *The Challenge of Jesus*, SPCK, 2000, p. 21.

7 Ibid., p. 90.

8 N. T. Wright, *Jesus and the Victory of God*, SPCK, 1996, p. 653.

9 Wright, *Challenge of Jesus*, p. 45.

10 See Luke 19:41–44. In Luke's account of the entry into Jerusalem, Jesus' weeping over the city and his cleansing the temple follow one another in a continuous narrative. It is the same in Matthew: Jesus goes straight to the temple, linking these two powerful prophetic signs. In Mark's account the cleansing of the temple happens the next day.

11 See 'An Order for the Beginning of Lent', in *Lent, Holy Week and Easter, Services and Prayers, Commended by the House of Bishops of the General Synod of the Church of England*, Church House Publishing / Cambridge University Press / SPCK, 1984, pp. 14–15.

12 Robert Warren, *Living Well*, HarperCollins, 1998, p. 85.

13 Sr Donna Marie McGargill, 'Servant Song', words and music, OCP Publications, 1984, published in *New Songs of Celebration*, McCrimmon Publishing, 1989.

14 To understand what it meant to be a disciple of Christ, I have written about Peter's journey at greater length in my book *On This Rock*, Bible Reading Fellowship, 2003.

15 Ibid., p. 93.

16 See Warren, *Living Well*, pp. 21–8.

17 Eric Milner-White, 'Self-Examination', in his *My God, My Glory*, SPCK, 1954, p. 23.

18 Milner-White, 'A Brief General Confession', in *My God, My Glory*, p. 26.

19 Told by Henri Nouwen, *Seeds of Hope*, Darton, Longman and Todd, 1989, pp. 124–5.

20 Augustine, *The SPCK Book of Christian Prayer*, SPCK, 1995, p. 247.

Chapter 4. The Tenacity of Love

1 Bob Smalhout, 'What killed Christ on the cross?' *Sunday Times*, 7 April 1985.

2 I have used this analogy for understanding the cross in my book *On This Rock*, Bible Reading Fellowship, 2003, p. 101.

3 Julian of Norwich, *Revelations of Divine Love*, trans. Clifton Wolters, Penguin Books, 1966, p. 100.

4 Ibid.

5 Ibid., pp. 108–9.

6 N. T. Wright, *The Challenge of Jesus*, SPCK, 2000, p. 69.

7 *The Mystery of Salvation: The Story of God's Gift*, a report by the Doctrine Commission of the General Synod of the Church of England, Church House Publishing, 1995, p. 198.

8 Ibid., p. 199.

9 Julian of Norwich, *Divine Love*, pp. 211–12.

10 Jeffrey John, *The Meaning in the Miracles*, Canterbury Press, 2001, pp. 162–3.

11 In this form found in *Common Worship: Services and Prayers for the Church of England, Pastoral Services*, Church House Publishing, 2000.

12 Quoted in Kenneth Leech, *True God*, Sheldon Press, 1985, p. 321. Also quoted in John, *Meaning in the Miracles*, p. 163.

13 Henri Nouwen, *Letters to Marc about Jesus*, Darton, Longman and Todd, 1988, p. 48.

14 Nelson Mandela, *Long Walk to Freedom*, Little, Brown, 1994, p. 319.

15 Ibid., pp. 613, 617.

16 *The SPCK Book of Christian Prayer*, SPCK, 1995, p. 128.

17 Ibid., p. 130.

18 For further discussion and practical help in everyday prayer, see my *Praying through Life*, Church House Publishing, 1998.

19. Hilary of Poitiers, *The SPCK Book of Christian Prayer*, p. 39.

20. Martin L. Smith SSJE, *Love Set us Free*, Cowley Publications, 1998, p. 48.

21 Catherine of Siena, *SPCK Book of Christian Prayer*, p. 38.

Chapter 5. Enduring Thirst

1 Author's adaptation to the NRSV.

2 Henri Nouwen, *Seeds of Hope*, Darton, Longman and Todd, 1989, p. 180.

3 Reported in the *Guardian*, 'One generation to save the world', 9 January 2003.

4 In what follows I have gathered information from the WaterAid website (www.wateraid.com), accessed 2 June 2003; from a *Church Times* supplement on water, 2 August 2002; and from a John Vidal article in the *Guardian* Earth supplement, August 2002.

5 *Church Times*, 2 August 2002.

6 From the WaterAid website (see note 3 above), and also the *Church Times*, 2 August 2002.

7 Adapted from '50 easy ways to save the planet', in the *Guardian* Earth supplement, August 2002, and Polly Toynbee, 'The lazy person's guide to saving the planet', *Guardian*, 29 August 2001.

8 Robert Warren, *Living Well*, HarperCollins, 1998, pp. 81–2.

9 Story told by Anthony de Mello, *The Song of the Bird*, Image Books, 1982, p. 153.

10 Prayer of the World Council of Churches in *The SPCK Book of Christian Prayer*, 1995, p. 263.

Chapter 6. Living Water

1 The fish was used probably because some of the first prominent disciples were fishermen, but also because the letters of the word 'fish' in Greek (*ichthys*) formed an acrostic for the first letters of a simple credal statement – 'Jesus Christ, God's Son, Saviour' – which the first Christians may well have memorized and used in teaching the faith.

2 William Temple, *Readings in St John's Gospel*, Macmillan, 1939, p. 59.

3 Ibid., p. 60.

4 I am indebted to Temple, *St John's Gospel*, pp. 63–8, for the insights explored here.

5 Apostolic Exhortation of Paul VI, *On Evangelization in the Modern World*, Pauline Books and Media, 1975, p. 9.

6 *Common Worship, Services and Prayers for the Church of England*, Church House Publishing, 2000, p. 353.

7 Author's adaptation to the NRSV.

8 Cited in Kenneth Leech, *Spirituality and Pastoral Care*, Sheldon Press, 1986, p. 131.

9 Temple, *St John's Gospel*, p. 67.

10 Henri Nouwen, *Seeds of Hope*, Darton, Longman and Todd, 1989, pp. 119–21.

11 H. Bonar, *The English Hymnal*, Oxford University Press, 1933, p. 747.

12 *Lent, Holy Week and Easter, Services and Prayers, Commended by the House of Bishops of the General Synod of the Church of England*, Church House Publishing / Cambridge University Press / SPCK, 1984, p. 235.

We want to hear from you. Please send your comments about this book to us in care of zreview@zondervan.com. Thank you.

GRAND RAPIDS, MICHIGAN 49530 USA

WWW.ZONDERVAN.COM